Late-summer flowering plants add seasonal interest to the more structural planting of this garden in the Midlands.

Previous page: A low-allergen garden created for the RHS Chelsea Flower Show in 1994 where the colour scheme of purple and pink extended to the paving, pots, fence, flowers and even the vegetables.

The Basics of PLANTING DESIGN

Lucy Huntington

PACKARD PUBLISHING LIMITED
CHICHESTER

The Basics of PLANTING DESIGN

© 2013 Lucy Huntington

First published in 2013 by Packard Publishing Limited, Forum House, Stirling Road, Chichester, West Sussex PO19 7DN, United Kingdom.

All photographs, line drawings and plans in the text are taken or drawn by the Author, who asserts her rights as the originator of the text and illustrations in this book.

All other rights are reserved. No part of this publication may be reproduced, stored in a retrieval system, transmitted in any form or by any means, electronic, mechanical, photocopying, recording or otherwise without either the written permission of the Publisher or a licence permitting restricted copying issued by the Copyright Licensing Agency, or its national equivalents throughout the world. This book may not be lent, resold, hired out or otherwise disposed of by way of trade in any form other than that in which was originally published without the prior permission of the Publisher.

ISBN: 978 185341 144 1

Front-cover photo taken by the Autor.
All line drawings, plans and photographs in the text are by the Author, unless where indicated otherwise.

Edited and prepared for press by Michael Packard.

Designed by Hilite Design & Reprographics Limited, Marchwood, Southampton, Hampshire.

Printed and bound in the United Kingdom by PublishPoint, Knowledgepoint Limited, Winnersh, Wokingham, Berkshire.

Dedication

To my grandchildren Arthur, Amelia and Evan, who constantly tell me to stop looking at flowers and remind me to have fun.

Acknowledgements

I am indebted to all my clients over the last forty years, who have allowed me the pleasure of helping them with their gardens, and particularly to the owners of the gardens which have provided the illustrations for this book;

And to Michael Packard, who encouraged me finally to get this book written, which I had been trying to do for the last twenty-five years.

I also need to acknowledge my past and present students, who have challenged me on the subject of planting design, which hopefully now has led to further clarification of the subject.

Finally, my thanks go to my husband Francis for his patience and constant support.

LH

CONTENTS

Preface

1 The Design Process 1
The design process 3
The client brief 3
The site survey 3
The functional plan 4
Functional planting 5
   Screen planting 6
   Protection from the wind 7
   Shade 7
   Noise reduction 7
   Food plants 7
The presentation plan – design principles 8
Harmony 9
Composition 10
Summary – design principles 11

2 The Use of Plants in Design 13
Structural planting 13
Ground-cover planting 16
   Formal ground cover 16
   Informal ground-cover planting 18
   Natural ground-cover planting 20
Focal-point planting 22
Ornamental planting 24
Summary 25

3 Planning Planted Areas 27
Factors to be considered 27
Sizes of planted areas 27
   Functional planting 27
   Screen planting 27
   Noise reduction 28
   Food plants 29
Structural planting 30
   Hedges 30
   Native hedges 30
   Avenues 32
Ground-cover planting 33

Focal-point planting 33
Ornamental planting 34
   Beds versus borders 34

4 The Visual Qualities of Plants 1 37
Shape 37
   Round or spherical 37
   Dome, bell 38
   Oval, columnar 39
   Cone, fan, square, spiky, tabular 41
Flower shapes 42
   Daisy, saucer, fleur-de-lis 42
   Fruit shape 42
Habit 43
   Weeping 43
   Pendulous, arching, upright 44
   Horizontal, tortuous 45
   Prostrate 46
Habits of leaves & flowers 46
Using shape & habit in planting design 47
Texture 47
   Size – fine, medium, bold 48
Shape of leaf 48
   Surface features 48
Summary – Using texture in design 49

5 The Visual Qualities of Plants 2 51
Colour spectrum 51
Colour harmonics 51
   Adjacent colours 51
   Opposite or complementary colours 55
   Tints, tones & shades 56
   Triads 56
Use of white in planting plans 58
Effects of seasons & sunlight 59
Natural colour harmonies 60
Playing with colour harmonies 61
Size 62
Using size 62
   Small, medium, large 63

6 Plant Selection 65
Trees 65
   Tree belts, structural groups, focal points 65
   Arboreta 66
   Orchards 67
Conifers 67
   Native, dwarf 67
   Medium-sized, large 68
Shrubs 69
   Evergreen 69
   Focal points 70
Hedges 70
   Native, boundary 70
   Internal division, informal flowering 70
   Ornamental 71
Climbers 71
Roses 72
   Species, shrub, bedding 73
   Planning rose beds 74
   English, climbing, ramblers 74
Ground cover 75
Herbaceous perennials 76
   Front-of-border plants 76
   Middle-of-bed plants 77
   Taller (back of border) plants 77
   Grasses & sedges 78
   Summary of shade plants 78
   Summary of ferns 79
Bulbs 79
Annuals & biennials 79
Listing possible plants 80
Plant associations 80

7 Planting Plans 83
Scales to use 83
Drawing planting plans 83
   Use of circles, naming plants 84
   Naming plants on the planting plan 84
Plant spacings 86
   Summary & notes on spacing 87

Working without planting plans	88	
Style & pattern of planting	88	
Formal, informal, drifts	89	
Placing plants on the plan	89	
Proposed plant list for a ground-cover bed	90	
Stages in preparing a planting plan	91	
Plant lists	93	
Plant list for a ground-cover bed	93	
Planting specifications & British Standards	93	
Summary to achieve successful planting	94	

Book list — 95

Index — 97

Plant list — 99

Figures

1.1	The client checklist	3
1.2	Survey of a narrow London garden	4
1.3	Functional plan of the same garden ...	4
1.4	Presentation plan	8
2.1	Planting to delineate spaces	14
2.2	Planting to reinforce a vista or axis	15
2.3	Planting to provide a background	23
4.1	Shapes found in plants – round to columnar	38
4.2	Shapes found in plants – cone to tabular	40
4.3	Habits of plants	43
5.1	The spectrum – showing primary, secondary and intermediate colours	52
7.1	Box in the corner of planting plan	84
7.2	Circles on planting plans	84
7.3	An intelligible planting plan	85
7.4	Another unintelligible plan	85
7.5	Part of a planting plan for streamside beds	86
7.6	The 1:3:5 rule for grouping plants	89
7.7	Part of a planting plan showing plants arranged in groups of 1, 3 and 5	89

Stages in preparing a planting plan for a ground-cover bed:

7.8	Stage 1 – fill an outline with circles ...	91
7.9	Stage 2 – link circles in drifts ...	91
7.10	Stage 3 – add plant names and quantities ...	91
7.11	Planting plan for a yellow and blue border	92

Boxed summaries and key information

Considerations for a functional plan	4
Summary of the design process	11
Summary – the selection and use of plants	25
Widths for screen planting	27
Shelter belts	28
Width of hedges	30
Native hedge species	31
Trees which make attractive avenues	32
Widths indicating potential planting for beds and borders	35
Sizes of leaf	48
Leaf sizes, surface features and margins	48
Use of colour in planting design	62
Plant sizes and usage	63
British native deciduous trees	65
Trees to use as focal points	66
Conifers which make good focal points	69
Evergreen shrubs for structural planting	69
Shrubs which make good focal points	70
Climbers	72

Ground-cover plants suitable for drifts	75
Native plants for wetland conditions	76
Front-of-border plants	76
Middle-of-bed or border plants	77
Back-of-border plants	77
Grasses	78
Sedges	78
Herbaceous plants for shade	78
Ferns	79
The identification box on a planting plan	81
Plant spacings	87
Planting styles and patterns	88
Proposed plant list and quantities for A ground-cover bed	91
Summary – how to achieve successful planting	94

PREFACE

This small book is a distillation of the knowledge I have gained from forty years of designing and planting gardens and twenty-five years of teaching garden and planting design.

I started formulating my approach to planting when I was asked in 1984 to teach a ten-week course on planting design for garden designers. Having accepted with alacrity, I started to look for books on planting design and found virtually nothing that would help. The few tomes that were available concentrated on planting the wider landscape as opposed to gardens, and used too much design jargon to be easily understandable. So I sat down and looked at how I chose and placed plants within a landscape or garden plan, and analysed my thought processes. Then I produced a lesson plan so that my students could understand and use the same process.

I began by looking at my designs, and then worked out how I decided where to use plants in my design as opposed to hard landscaping or water. I then separated out the ways in which I used plants into structural, ground-cover, ornamental and focal-point planting; it was only later that I added functional planting, first for vegetable gardens and then later for shelter and screening plants.

When it came to the visual qualities of individual plants, I used the book on planting design written by my former Professor, Brian Hackett, to help me with a list of shapes and habits. For colour I went back to the books by Faber Birren and Johannes Itten, and using their ideas as a basis, I looked at how the changing light, changing seasons and prevalence of green affected the use of colour harmonies in the landscape. Penelope Hobhouse's excellent book *Colour in Your Garden* was published in the year after I started refining my ideas, but it was a great resource for later lectures. I have never found a good resource book on texture and have largely expressed my own ideas on this key subject.

When it came to drawing planting plans I was adamant, and remain so, that plans should be clear, accurate and unambiguous so that whoever does the planting places each plant exactly where the designer intends it to go. I eschewed the existing books on planting plans written for landscape architects because they contained elegant plans which were, in my opinion, unintelligible to the contractor. It is pure arrogance and stupidity on the part of the designer to create plans that a contractor cannot read.

Another area that needed clarification was plant spacing, since there was no clear guide on this subject. The guidelines I first set out on this topic are still those I use today.

Over the past twenty-five years I have continued to use most of the original handouts I created all those years ago, albeit with some minor changes. When reviewing them now, they still hold true despite the changes in planting styles and the availability of a much wider range of plants in a greater assortment of sizes.

The material in this book will be very familiar to my past students, but it should serve as a refresher course for them; they will notice a change of emphasis in one or two areas. For those people who are unfamiliar with my thoughts on planting, I hope that this book will prove to be a useful addition to their libraries.

LH

A pair of oval-shaped shrubs (Phillyrea angustifolia) *placed to enhance a focal point.*

1 THE DESIGN PROCESS

So what is planting design and why do I consider it so important? Put quite simply it is the selection and use of plants to achieve the designer's intended design objectives. The reason it is so important is that there is so little good planting design around. There are plenty of new interesting planting ideas, and there are some good examples of planted areas to go and look at, but what is lacking is an overall understanding of the totality of planting design.

Advocates of new schools of planting will make derogatory remarks about what they consider to be old-fashioned planting ideas, and there seems to be a plethora of information about new wave plantings – new naturalism, prairie planting and so forth – without putting these into the context of their surroundings. Many landscape courses still put planting design at the bottom of the agenda, and consider plant knowledge to be almost unnecessary so long as some sort of plant database is available. Students may produce exciting designs and lots of detail about the hard landscaping, only to use plants just to add some 'greening' to their projects. They may use, at best, a list of acceptable plants and at worst a list of unsuitable, unattractive and unobtainable plants. I do not mean to be impolite or reactionary, but these observations reflect the experience of being an external examiner for various courses on many occasions.

A low-allergen garden for the Royal Horticultural Society's Chelsea Flower Show where the colour scheme of yellow and blue-purple was followed in the trellis, the artefacts and the flower colours.

The problem may be that planting design is among the hardest of all design disciplines to do really well. There are so many factors to be considered:

- *Designs are three-dimensional* because they are intended to be walked through and round, so that one can look at them from all sides both at a distance and close up;

- *Design will change with the seasons* and the years, and is subject to varying light conditions;

- *The materials used are living,* and therefore at one extreme can die, and at the other may survive, but to grow really well, need to be maintained correctly;

- *It takes many years of study to acquire a working knowledge* of the wide choice of plants that are available.

I do not believe that there is any other form of design in which there are so many variables or potential problems. However, to counteract the negatives, the material we use is intrinsically attractive and, so long as the plants selected are appropriate for the soil, aspect and drainage of the site, the result should be a planting that looks good and grows well. Our planting design may well be 'good enough' but not outstanding, and even then many people would not know the difference between what has been presented and what could have been achieved.

A narrow path leads into the garden and around the planting.

In many cases, however, particularly in urban landscaping, the plants are not well chosen for either the site or the available maintenance. In order to achieve an instant effect they are usually planted far too densely and, within a few years, the result is either a tangled mess of foliage, or a desert of trampled ground with a few struggling plants. I often despair at the phenomenal wastage of good plant material when I see these results. A lack of understanding of design within the garden will result in borders full of colour for short periods, which then suffer for many months with nothing interesting to look at.

Another problem is that, particularly in garden design, selecting and placing plants is often the most time-consuming part of the design process and yet, because plants may be the least expensive part of creating a garden, we feel that we cannot charge clients as much for a planting plan as for an overall or presentation plan. I have been producing planting plans for clients for over 35 years and it is still the most demanding part of many of my projects. At least I do now get paid for the time I take — or I do in most cases — and this is probably due to the fact that I am now much quicker at producing plans while my knowledge and experience continue to grow. However, I hope that by reading this workbook, you may find it easier and faster to produce good planting design and workable planting plans.

The design process

Planting design is an integral part of any design for an open space, be it hectares of landscaping or a small town garden. The process starts right from the outset of the project. When designers survey sites and receive their briefings, they should be looking at their projects in terms of how designs might evolve using the range of materials they have at their disposal. These elements include landform, water, hard landscaping and plants. While the first concepts of the overall design emerge, certain decisions will be made as to how the lines and shapes of the design will be created. Should a line be vertical or horizontal and, if vertical, is it a wall, a fence, a hedge or a row of trees? Is a horizontal space to be paving, water or grass?

It is now worth going through the whole design process step by step, and to look at where and how we can use planting design to help push the developing plans along.

The client brief

The first stage of any design is the client brief, when clients provide their input into how they would like their site designed. These preferences may involve major design limitations or include specific features. The briefing may also consider plants and required planting areas. The designer also needs to know about possible planning restrictions on the site, and any below-ground services. A budget for construction and planting, as well as for future maintenance, should be agreed. However well thought out and executed a planting plan is, if there is inadequate maintenance, the planting will fail. As with all the different forms of art, planting design is most reliant on being looked after properly.

The site survey

A site needs to be surveyed after receipt of the client brief. This again may dictate how plants will be used, as the designer will be checking the soil, aspect and microclimates within the site, and the drainage. It is impossible to create good planting design without understanding the importance of these factors when selecting plants that will grow and survive. On larger sites where there is existing native vegetation, an appreciation of ecology will help decide which additional plants are appropriate. It may indeed be a condition of the project that only native plants are used and in ecologically sound groupings.

The Client Checklist

Use of garden
Outside room	– need for terrace	Entertainment	– barbecue	Relaxation	– absence of noise
Children	– age/safety	Sports	– tennis/swimming	Food production	– fruit/vegetables
Growing plants	– see list	Wild life	– pond/birds	Other uses	_____

Functional Requirements
access and parking	___	screening	___	shelter	___	white noise	___
garden furniture	___	greenhouse	___	shed	___	play equipment	___
vegetable garden	___	fruit cage	___	compost Heap	___	oil tank	___
log store	___	wheelie bins	___	lighting	___	other	_____

Style of garden   formal ___   informal ___   wild ___

Plants/planted areas to include
trees	___	avenue	___	arboretum	___	tree belt	___
shrubs	___	hedges	___	roses	___	rose garden	___
climbers	___	conifers	___	herbs	___	ferns	___
formal lawn	___	grass for play	___	long grass w. bulbs	___	meadow	___
ground cover	___	beds & borders	___	plants with scent	___	bedding	___t
bamboos	___	grasses	___	potager	___	orchard	___
bee plants	___	butterfly plants	___	plants for birds	___		
Favourite plants	_____						
Favourite colours	_____						

Garden features to include
water		pergola	___	trellis	___	summerhouse	

Maintenance   family ___   gardener ___   hours available ___

Budget   £_____

Figure 1.1 Client checklist

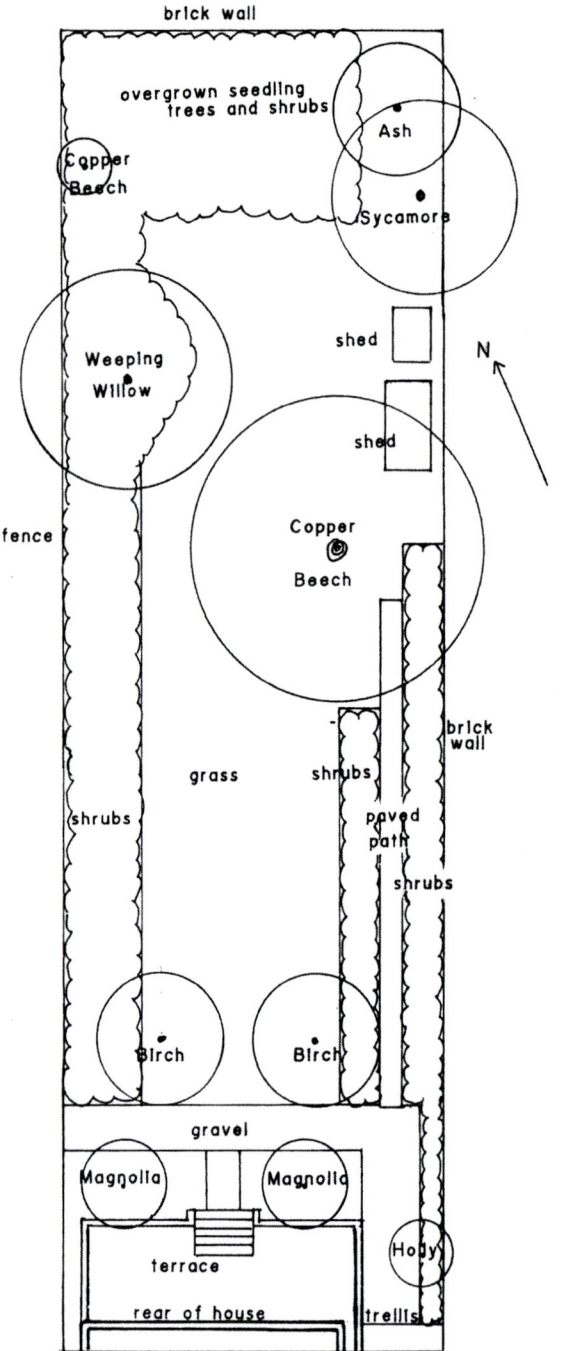

Figure 1.2 *Survey of a narrow London garden.*

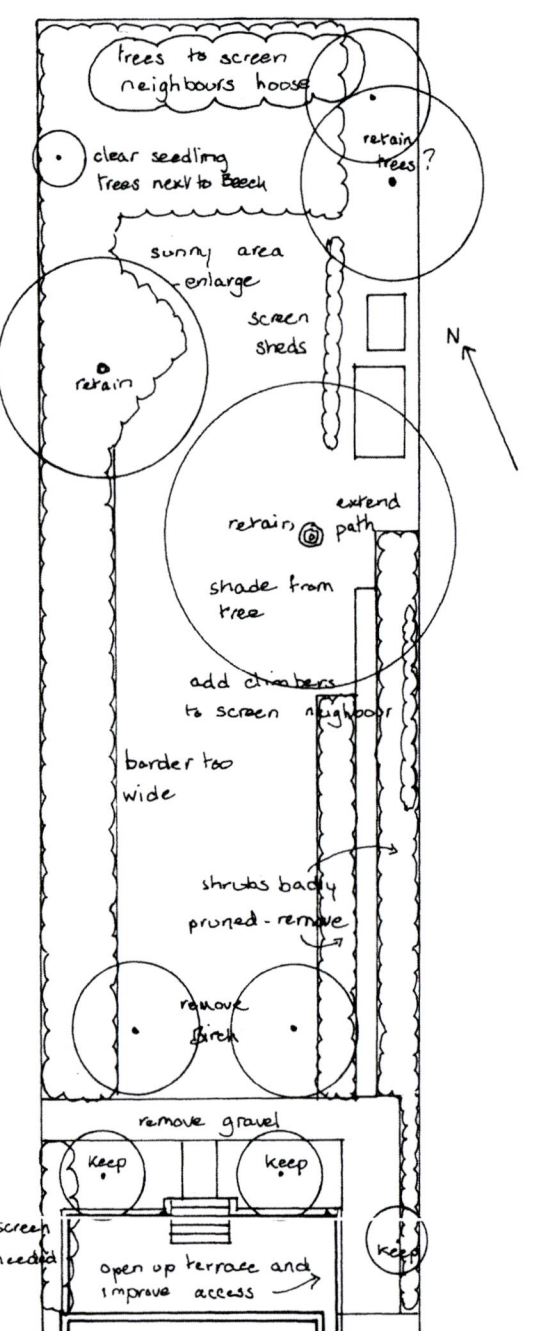

Figure 1.3 *Functional plan of the same garden; this is drawn over the survey.*

The survey is also the stage at which the wise designer consults the 'genius loci' or the spirit of the place. This may sound a bit far-fetched, but it has been an essential part of the design process for at least the last 2000 years. Put simply, it is allowing oneself to feel the qualities of the space, perhaps by noting areas which are more exposed, areas of stillness, potential sun-traps, and to note who and what is already occupying the site and whose habitats need to be respected. I have found that it is often this stage which provides the clue to some of my more successful designs.

The functional plan

Once the briefing data have been collected, a site survey is drawn up and the design stage begins. But before getting on with creating a composition with pattern and line, the functional considerations need to be considered. Any, or all, of the following may need to be addressed:

- access into and around the site;
- provision for parking;
- security of the site, including lighting;
- proposed activity areas;
- areas exposed to the wind which need shelter;
- unattractive views within and without the site boundaries;
- planning conditions that need to be respected.

Once decisions have been made about these issues, a functional plan emerges, which will include existing planting to be retained, and areas for functional planting indicated.

Functional planting

When assessing a site, the designer needs to look at practical and legal requirements that may be resolved by the use of plants. They are not part of the design at this stage, but need to be indicated on the functional plan. How to incorporate these plantings into the overall design can then be decided.

The previous section outlines the functional requirements which may be solved practically. If there is any development on the site, there may be legally binding planning requirements in terms of screening proposed buildings, planting new boundaries or adding trees to replace those removed for the development.

The clients also may have specific requirements which need to be located at this 'functional plan' stage, such as the need for a vegetable garden.

Types of functional planting:
1. Screen planting,
2. Protection from wind,
3. Shade,
4. Noise reduction,
5. Food plants.

A formal vegetable garden is surrounded by box hedging and espalier fruit trees.

A hornbeam hedge provides an effective screen for the vegetable garden behind.

A view of cottages before planting a screening tree belt.

The choice of plants for functional planting is quite limited as they need to be:

- usually trees or shrubs;
- evergreen where possible;
- able to thrive in the soil, aspect and drainage of the site;
- fast-growing and hardy;
- native species in most rural locations.

It may help to look at the different ways in which functional planting is used. I consider at least five types of functional planting.

1. Screen planting is used:

- to hide unwanted views;
- to obscure boundaries;
- to give privacy.

Hiding unwanted views

The view may be on or off site. Plants used for screening need to have green foliage with a fine or medium texture, so that the screen does not draw the eye but rather acts as a neutral background. Whether shrubs or trees are used will depend on the height of screen needed and the space available.

The view of the cottages three years after planting the tree belt.

To provide or obscure boundaries

At this stage it is important to note where the boundaries are on the site and to mark them accordingly. It may also be appropriate to show where any boundary structures or planting should be replaced, and any need for greater definition of the boundaries. Hedges are often used for boundaries, and the choice of species will depend on the site of the garden or open space. Open spaces in rural areas will frequently have mixed native hedges, and rural estates may have tree belts along part of their boundaries to act as wind protection, but also to leave it unclear as to how far the land extends.

Privacy

Most people need some privacy within their gardens, as well as around them, and this may be indicated on the functional plan at this stage. Design ideas also may need to be developed before addressing this issue. Screen planting may then be used to create the desired level of privacy.

2. Protection from wind

The best protection from wind is a permeable barrier which breaks the force of the wind rather than stopping it completely. If stopped, the wind will flow over the barrier and can cause turbulence when it reaches the ground on the leeward side. In many cases a hedge is used, but for larger spaces a tree belt can be more effective both visually and in the amount of protection it gives. Wind-resistant species need to be used in areas where there is a high level of wind exposure; where the site is exposed to sea winds, the species need to be salt tolerant.

3. Shade

Shade may be a consideration particularly where the site is fully exposed to the sun. In warmer and sunnier climates this may be the first consideration in the planning process. Instant shade can be provided by providing walls and fences, or for greater height a pergola covered with climbers. If there are existing trees on site, which could be used for shade, they may be worth retaining almost regardless of what they look like. Another more attractive tree can then be planted which will create shade in the future, and the original tree or trees felled in due course.

4. Noise reduction

Many sites will have busy roads adjacent to their boundaries and, depending on the volume of passing traffic, there may be a requirement to try to reduce the road noise within the site. There have been some interesting studies on the subject of plants and noise reduction, and the main finding was that any form of planted barrier will help to lower the volume. Dense coniferous hedges would seem to be the best planting for this purpose. Where there is room a good alternative is an earth-bank with a dense hedge planted on top.

5. Food plants

These may include both vegetables and fruit and need to be placed where they will grow well; nearly all vegetables require good deep soil, full sun and beds that are easy to manage. As they are functional areas they need to be planned as such. This may mean that they need to be screened from the rest of the garden. Fruit trees may be in the form of cordons used to screen the vegetable garden, or vines on a pergola. An orchard or individual fruit trees can be included within the general tree planting plan. They need good soil, full sun for ripening fruit, and to be planted above any potential frost pockets. Decisions about, and positioning of, food plants needs to be part of the functional planning stage as they may well impose limits on the overall design.

The presentation plan – design principles

The next stage is to produce outline or presentation plans. An outline can be used to show clients design ideas; a presentation plan will show the final layout, and may possibly be coloured. This is the stage when the design actually starts, and the designer needs to incorporate the two great principles of harmony and composition. There is not enough space in this book to explain these two principles in any detail but there are many books now available on the subject. Because I will be referring to these principles in the following chapters, I will give only a brief outline here on how I interpret and use harmony and composition to create my designs.

Notes to Figure 1.4:
1. Garden planned to be in three areas: formal garden, rose garden and woodland garden.
2. Painted trellis and arches between formal garden and rose garden.
3. Yew hedge between rose garden and woodland garden.
4. Formal garden: 4 no. *Malus trilobata* against side fence, 5 no. *Photinia x fraseri* 'Red Robin' above terrace to screen neighbour.
5. Rose garden: roses selected which tolerate some shade; yew hedge on either side of garden, stone benches either side of statue.
6. Woodland garden: 4 no. *Carpinus betulus* 'Fastigiata' planted at northern end to screen neighbour; new trees chosen for blossom and autumn colour; mown grass path to separate two areas of longer grass with bulbs.
7. Sheds screened with *Carpinus betulus* hedge.
8. Existing paved path to side retained and extended to join new paved area by house.

The London garden shown in the presentation plan three months after completion of the planting.

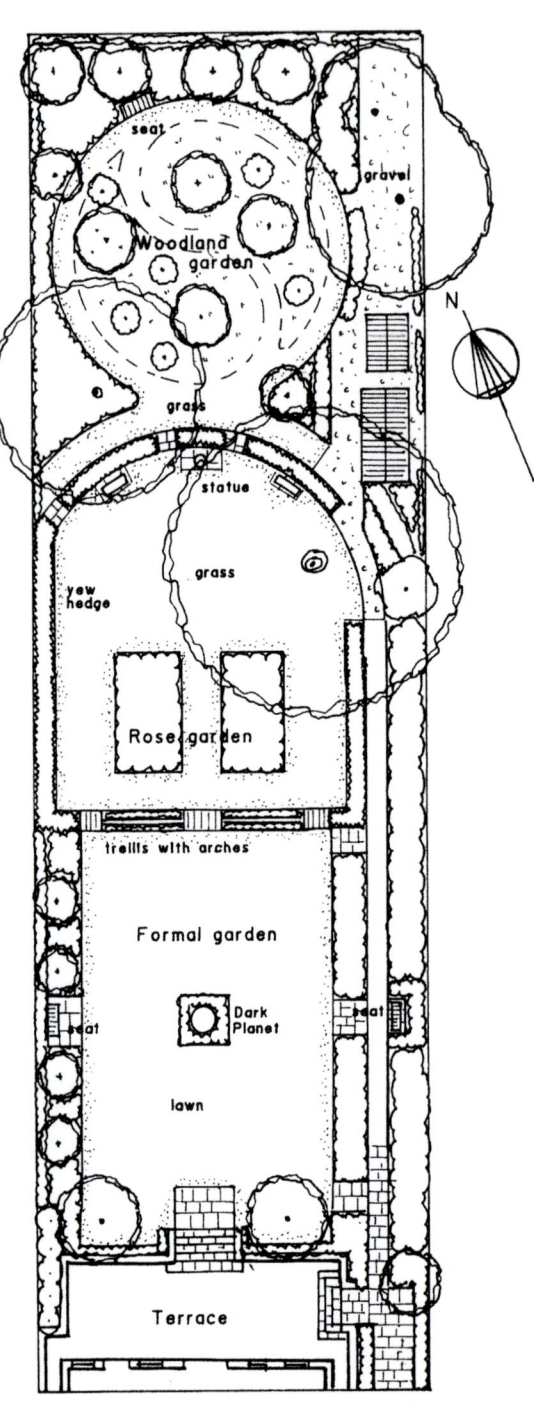

Figure 1.4 Presentation plan.

Harmony

No designer can work successfully without understanding the need for harmony, even if they then include its opposite, discord, to stimulate the senses. Harmony gives a sense that everything belongs together, and forms a connected and related whole. It engenders a feeling of peace within the onlooker. It is the element that is most often lacking in many gardens where no conscious thought has been given to whether the various elements of the garden belong together.

Harmony can be achieved by the two related concepts of unity and simplicity:

Unity can be interpreted as oneness, a coherence of all the parts that make up the whole. It can be achieved by using the same range of hard-landscaping materials, using the same or related shapes whether formal or informal, and using plants with similar physical needs and related visual qualities.

Simplicity means keeping it simple, by limiting the features, materials and plants used, and lots of repetition.

Harmony is also affected by the use of scale and proportion, and these elements need to relate to each other. Within the context of the site and the buildings, the designer needs

Simple planting along a stream using plants that enjoy damp soil and with an overall yellow and green colour scheme.

to select the scale to be used; for example a large open space needs a large scale, a large country garden a medium scale, and a town garden a small scale. Once the scale is chosen, then all the elements used need to be in proportion. The open space will need wide paths, large trees and extensive planted areas, whereas the country garden needs paths of standard width, medium-sized trees and reasonably large flower beds and borders. The town garden needs narrow paths, small trees and small beds and borders. Once skilled in design, a designer can use a change in proportion to produce excitement, but only when the importance of scale and proportion is fully understood; otherwise the design just looks odd.

Composition

Composition is the art of creating pictures that draw the eye and allow the viewer to appreciate what has been created. The centre of any composition is the focal point which is a feature or group of features that stand out from their surroundings and invite the eye to stop and enjoy the picture. Typical focal points in a garden might be a summer-house, a large tree, a gate, a fountain, a seat or a statue. Where no thought has been given to composition, it may be a greenhouse, the compost heap or a washing line! To enjoy the focal point the eye needs to have a clear line

A large country garden with extensive lawn, wide paths and borders.

of sight to it, and this is known as the axis or vista and should describe a straight line from the intended viewpoint to the focal feature. Further enhancement of the focal point can add to its impact, and might include a suitable base and background with some supporting features at either side. The summer-house would be enhanced by laying paving in front, by planting a background of evergreen shrubs or by adding a plant either side of its doors. The axis can also be visually strengthened by adding supporting features like an avenue of trees either side, or a canal of water down the centre.

A garden or landscape may be a single composition, or a series of compositions with openings between that draw the visitor around the space in turn presenting each composition to be enjoyed. A composition may be as simple as a field gate at the end of an avenue or as complicated as a series of waterfalls with surrounding features and vegetation.

A small garden with small lawn, narrow paths and borders.

Summary of the design process

1. Visit new client — client briefing; complete check-list.
2. Site survey — collect data and explore 'genius loci'.
3. Analyse data and draw up survey — add functional requirements.
4. The Functional Plan — add functional planting:
   - screen planting;
   - shelter from wind;
   - shade;
   - noise reduction;
   - food plants.
5. Draw up Outline Plan — add design ideas, using the design principles:
   - harmony;
   - composition;
   - scale and proportion.
6. Visit client — show outline plan with ideas, revisit checklist.
7. Complete Presentation Plan and present to client.

When I first visited this garden there was an unmowable grass slope between the terrace and the lower lawn. The slope was eliminated by building two dwarf walls to create a 6000mm terrace which is planted with parterres and colourful borders.

2 THE USE OF PLANTS IN DESIGN

As discussed in the last chapter, the designer decides where to use plants to create the design, and this decision depends on what part the plants are to play. Plants can be used structurally to create the lines, shapes and patterns of the design. They can be used as ground cover to clothe the horizontal surfaces. They may provide or support focal points, or used purely ornamentally to add interest and colour, often at a specific time of the year.

Each plant placed on a plan should have a specific part to play in the overall design of the garden or landscape. There is no room for dotting trees around or carelessly massing plants in borders. In the larger garden or landscape, plants may be the only material the designer will want to use, perhaps following the example of Lancelot Brown, who in the late eighteenth century created some of the best-loved landscapes using only trees, grass or water, with the occasional gravel path or drive. Conversely in a small town garden, the designer may rely on walls and paving for much of the design, with plants used more ornamentally to add seasonal colour and interest, and to soften the impact of the hard landscaping.

There are five ways in which we can use plants in our designs and these are:

1. **Functional planting,** which has been discussed in Chapter 1;
2. **Structural planting;**
3. **Ground-cover planting;**
4. **Focal-point planting;**
5. **Ornamental planting.**

Structural planting

Structural planting is about using plants to create the vertical lines and to outline the shapes, or forms, of a proposed design. It can be:

Planting to create lines;
Planting to delineate space;
Planting to reinforce axes.

The alternative materials for providing vertical lines and shapes are walls, fencing, trellis or landform.

Plants used for structural planting are visually the most important ones in terms of design, and need to be those that really thrive in the soil and local climate. Usually trees or shrubs are used for structural planting, and the easiest to establish and most likely to thrive will be the native plants of the area, provided that they are selected for the specific soil, aspect and drainage of the site.

Planting to create lines

In planting terms, vertical lines can be rows of trees or shrubs, or the edge of woodland. For more formal lines, one can use clipped hedges and avenues. Where space is limited, walls and fences may need a 'greener' look, so a combination of hard materials and planting may satisfy our design objectives. These include 'fedges', which are fences with a hedge planted in front. On sites where space is very restricted, a green vertical line can be created by using trellis and climbing plants; or the newer alternative of a 'green wall' can be used.

Planting to delineate space

This is planting used to outline the shapes that we have designed on the horizontal plane. Plants may provide an edging to the shape as a line, such as a hedge, or be the edge of a block of planting, for example a shrub border or a woodland copse. Lower containment of a shape may be provided by the line between mown and longer grass, or by the edge of a flower border. The relationship between the size of the horizontal space and the height of the surrounding structural planting will depend on the mood the designer wishes to engender in the viewer. At one extreme, a small space surrounded by tall plants can be exciting; at the other, a large space surrounded by low planting can be very peaceful. If one gets the proportions wrong, though, the first area will be frightening and the second boring.

Plan of a formal garden where planting in the form of hedges has been used to delineate the various garden areas

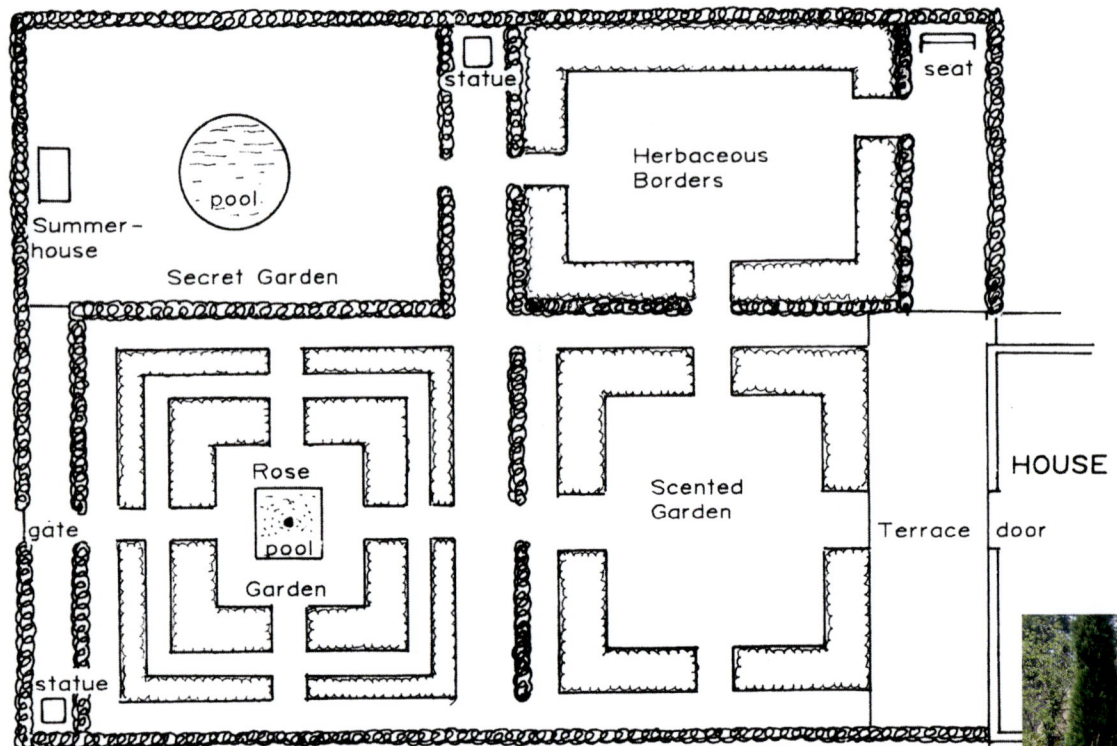

hedges used to delineate areas

Figure 2.1 Planting to delineate spaces.

Planting to reinforce axes

As mentioned in the previous chapter, all focal points need clearly defined axes, and these axes may need to be reinforced to give greater impact. We can use avenues of trees or shrubs, or we can outline the sides with hedges, blocks of woodland or the edge of parallel borders. If the garden is formal, parallel lines of clipped trees set at regular spaces may be most appropriate. In a more informal setting, it may be appropriate to have just trees or shrubs arranged on either side of the vista, but without rigid adherence to regular spacing. Alternatives to plants for reinforcing axes are pergolas, pillars, fences or walls.

Part of Withersdane Hall gardens which are divided into a series of seven areas by the use of yew hedges planted in the 1950s.

An avenue of pleached trees either side of the drive to the house.

The planting included at the functional planning stage needs to be addressed at this point, in order to see if it can also be used for structural planting. So boundary and screen planting may be used to help define a horizontal space. If so, the edge of the planting within the design area may describe a quite different outline to the line on the boundary.

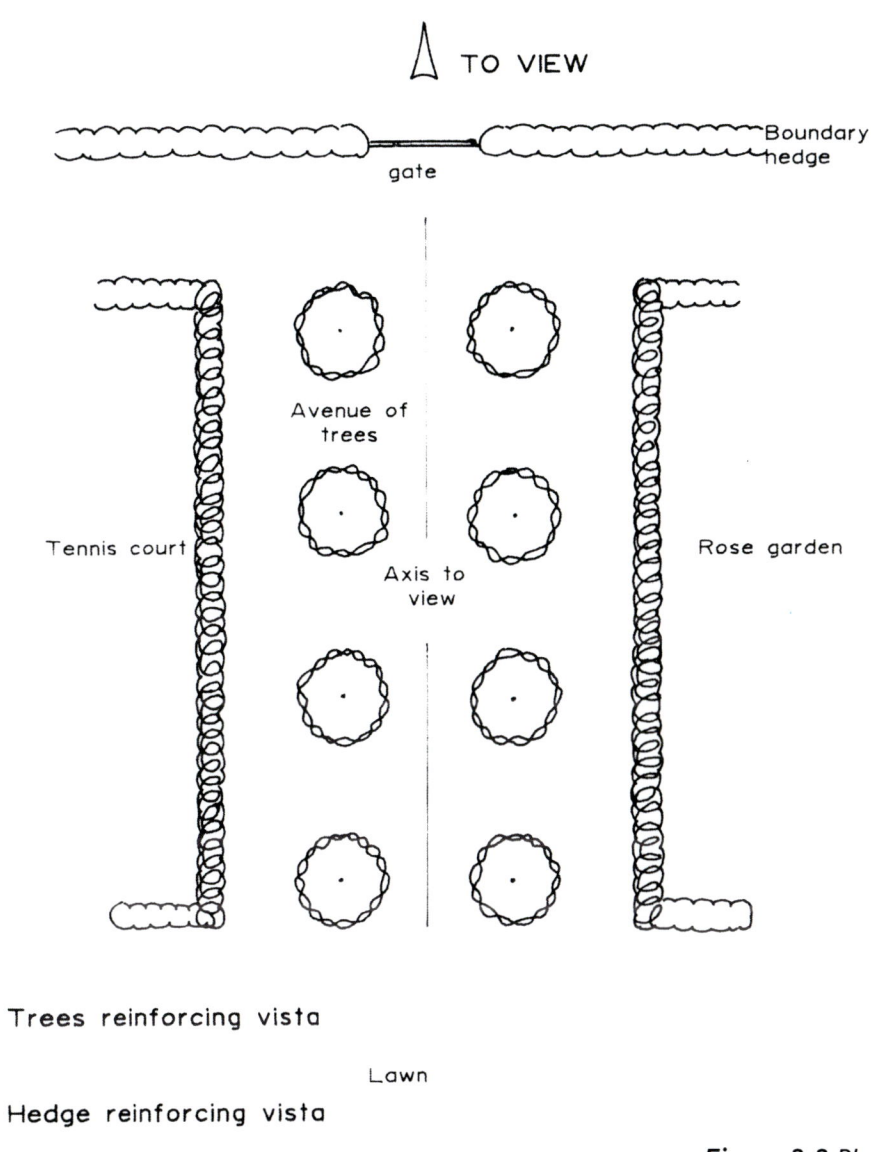

Figure 2.2 *Planting to reinforce a vista. Parallel hedges and an avenue of trees are used to direct the eye of the viewer to the view beyond.*

Ground-cover planting

This is the next area of planting that needs to be considered while developing our design ideas. Ground-cover planting is not just the use of specific ground-covering plants, but any type of planting used as horizontal cover or pattern. These are the plants that form the basis of gardens and landscapes. The most frequently used plants in Britain are grasses grown as a lawn or a mown-grass area. In other parts of the world, where grass does not grow so well, alternatives are used which usually have a similar visual impact to lawn grasses. The alternative materials to planting to cover the horizontal space are paving — particularly where there is heavy use — gravel, water or mulch.

In the context of planting design, ground-cover planting ranges from formal bedding at one extreme, to a carpet of woodland bluebells at the other, from intricate planting detail to swathes of a single plant.

We need to decide on whether we are going to use a formal, informal or a natural approach to the ground-cover areas. This decision will depend on the style of the garden, the client's wishes, and the amount of potential maintenance available. In larger schemes there may be areas of all three styles, ranging from formal areas near the buildings to informal beyond, and then natural areas as we near the boundaries.

Formal ground cover

Formal ground-cover planting is usually restricted to areas which are designed along formal lines, and it should reflect the outlines and shapes of the design. This use of ground cover includes:

- *Formal areas of mown grass,*
- *Carpet bedding,*
- *Parterres,*
- *Knot gardens,*
- *Formal beds of a single plant.*

Formal areas of mown grass are regularly shaped expanses of mown grass which are maintained using a cylinder mower with a roller on the back which creates the stripes which are a feature of this type of lawn. For the best effect, the area needs to have a formal shape to which the mowing stripes can relate visually. The grass mixture needs to include grasses which survive when cut at a low height. The person maintaining the area needs to understand the need for regular mowing plus feeding, scarifying and spiking. In cases where the client wants and understands the need for detailed lawn care, such lawns can look absolutely stunning. Unfortunately it is more usual that they are not maintained and can look weedy and uncared for. An easier approach is to have an area of grass which is cut with a rotary mower and left at a higher

A mown lawn showing the traditional striped effect created by a cylinder mower.

Carpet bedding at the Royal Horticultural Society's garden at Wisley.

A parterre in summer.

The same parterre (left) in winter.

Spring bedding used to add interest to a courtyard.

Formal squares of ground-cover plants, mulch and stone chippings.

level: not so stunning to look at, but much easier and cheaper to maintain. The designer has to decide at the planning stage which type of mown grass is most likely to look attractive within the constraints of the budget and maintenance.

Carpet bedding is the use of low bedding-plants placed in a formal pattern, which has the effect of adding colour and interest to a lawn area, much as a patterned rug does to a wooden floor or plain carpet. It was very popular with the Victorians and in municipal parks, and is still seen today. The shape of the area to be planted adds to the impact of the design and needs to reflect that shape, and to be in proportion to the area of surrounding grass. Less formal, but with the same 'patterned carpet' appearance, are formal beds of bedding plants arranged randomly.

Parterres are complicated patterns created with low box hedges, and were a feature of Italian Renaissance gardens, where they were planted in gravel, whereas in French formal gardens they were surrounded with grass. They create a textured-rug effect when used either in grass or paving, and have become popular recently. The complexity of the pattern is limited by the designer's creativity, the size of the area and the maintenance available.

Knot gardens are usually square patterns created with a mixture of low hedges which may include lavender, santolina, wall germander, box and, more recently, hebe. Traditionally found in English gardens in Elizabethan times, they have also enjoyed a renaissance in recent years. They are more difficult to maintain, as the various plants grow at different rates, and many are short-lived so may need replanting frequently. I find it easier to stick to the parterre approach just using box but keeping the pattern relatively simple.

Formal beds of a single plant are a more recent trend and often arranged asymmetrically. A variety of low-growing plants may be used to keep them in shape.

It is a matter of individual taste — the designer's or the client's — as to which form of planted 'rug' is considered the more acceptable and attractive.

Informal ground-cover planting

This includes:

- ***Informal areas of mown grass,***
- ***Drifts of ground-cover plants,***
- ***Longer grass with bulbs.***

Long grass forming the curving line encircling the mown grass.

Mown grass path between beds sown with a mixture of grasses and wild flowers.

Informal areas of mown grass are informally-shaped areas which are cut with a rotary mower without the stripy effect of formal lawns. In design terms, these grass areas can create many horizontal shapes, and are most effective when the shape is simple and mowable. At the outset it is important to decide how the shape is to be contained: by the edge of a bed, a block of shrubs and trees, a hedge or a wall. On a practical note, whenever the grass area is adjacent to a wall or fence, consideration needs to be given to providing a mowing strip to avoid unnecessary strimming at the edges. The mowing strip can be of bricks, paving, gravel (if left below grass level) or a single row of plants, but space for it needs to be included in the design.

Drifts of ground-cover plants

As already stated, grass species, due to the fact that they grow well in the soil and climate of the British Isles for example, often provide the easiest alternative but, not surprisingly there are areas where grass will not grow well. This may be due to shady conditions, excessive moisture or a logistical problem with mowing; in these circumstances, other plants which create a similar fine-leaved, green low cover can be used. A single, suitable species is selected and planted over the whole site. Other areas of ground-cover planting may add more interest and colour, in which case a range of suitable plants should be planted in drifts, blocks or randomly.

Areas of longer grass with bulbs are useful where the landscape or garden space exceeds the maintenance available or where there is a requirement for areas of naturalized bulbs. They are much easier to establish and maintain than wildflower meadows, as the bulbs come up before the grasses start growing in the spring, and die down just as the need to start mowing arises. Wildflower meadows are only suited to thin sandy or chalk soils, where the grasses do not grow well and the wild flowers have a chance to compete. I try to steer my clients away from the idea of wildflower meadows towards naturalized bulbs in long grass, unless the soil is really suitable for the former. In addition, with a heavy clay soil where grasses grow extremely well, I restrict the bulbs used to those which flower in the early spring to allow for an early cut of grass in late spring. Bulbs are always scattered randomly either in drifts of a single species or a simple mixture of species.

A bank of Lamium galeobdolon *used on an unmowable site.*

A bank planted with with grasses and rudbeckia at the London Olympic Park.

Naturalized daffodils making a wonderful display in spring.

Bluebells forming a natural ground cover in a beech wood.

Natural ground-cover planting

We can, of course, copy nature and use ground-cover plants which are native to the soil and the area. Much is written today about ecological planting, the ecological fit or creative ecology; all are basically looking at the native plants which would flourish in the prevailing conditions of a site, and then using them for our planting schemes. Such schemes should include the appropriate mix of trees and shrubs, as well as herbaceous plants and even annuals and biennials. Apart from the fact that these plants will grow well, they may also provide cover and possibly food for some of our native fauna. When planting ecologically, therefore, it is not just the ground cover that we need.

In Britain, I am familiar with the various ecological fits to be found on the different soils and locations, and instinctively I use this knowledge when planning my plantings. However, when I first started selecting plants for a site in Illinois, USA, which was surrounded by miles of ploughed fields, I realized that I had no knowledge of the natural ecology of the area, and I could not start until I had absorbed the relevant information.

There are five types of natural ground cover in Britain which may be appropriate to the sites we are designing, and these are:

- *Woodland,*
- *Woodland edge,*
- *Wetland,*
- *Downland,*
- *Moorland.*

Woodland is perhaps the easiest to plant in Britain, as all the countryside would have been covered originally by trees, and there is an extensive range of native woodland herbaceous plants from which to select those that are appropriate for the specific site being designed. One of the problems to face is that, if the trees are all recently planted, some of the deep woodland plants will not thrive initially. They will be needed later when the shade increases, so I tend to plant a mixture of woodland-edge and woodland plants, and let the plants themselves decide which of them is best suited to occupy the space. To begin with, the woodland-edge plants will be more aggressive but, as the tree canopy increases, the plants which tolerate the evolving shade will tend to dominate. This type of planting can be kept very simple with just drifts of bluebells, or can include a range of woodland species planted as a matrix or as drifts with standards.

Woodland edge is mentioned above and is the area where a wood meets the open countryside, and the plants which inhabit this area enjoy a mixture of sun and shade.

Wetlands cover a range of moisture levels from areas always covered by water, to those which are wet in winter and quite dry in summer. There are many lovely native plants for these areas, but they need to be selected for the moisture levels found on site. They usually occur as a mixture of different plants, but in quite large individual groupings, and the dividing line between the groups usually coincides with a change in the moisture level.

Downland is the nearest we have to a natural wildflower meadow. If the site has thin sandy or chalky soils, there is a real opportunity to establish a successful meadow using a seed mixture of native grasses and plants, and these will thrive on the specific soil conditions found on the site. Alternatively plugs of herbaceous plants can be planted randomly into an existing sward. There has been extensive work done recently on the suitable seed mixtures, so select a knowledgeable supplier.

Heathland occurs on thin acid soil and can be very dry or conversely quite boggy; again there is a range of suitable plants which can be used. Often these occur naturally in large drifts of a single plant rather than as a mixture. Heather moorlands are an example where *Calluna vulgaris* dominates.

There are two types of ***quasi-natural ground-cover planting***, that is planting which appears natural and may include native plants but is not ecologically correct. These have received a lot of media coverage, and have become very popular in recent years. These are:

Wildflower meadows

Unfortunately there has been much publicity given to this subject, and clients see such meadows as easy, and more decorative, alternatives to mown grass. They are not easy, because they do not occur naturally in Britain, and are extremely difficult to establish and maintain unless given very thin well-drained soils and planted as downland (see above). On sites where there is good topsoil, the grasses will always dominate, and eventually smother all the herbaceous plants except for a few thugs like yarrow (*Achillea millefolium*) and buttercup (*Ranunculus acris* & spp.).

Prairie planting originated in the mid-west of North America, and is a form of wildflower meadow with a combination of tall prairie grasses and associated herbaceous plants. I have used prairie planting as ground cover on the large estate in Illinois mentioned earlier, and it looked very attractive for the summer, but needed burning off in the autumn, after which the bare ground was covered by snow in the winter. The name 'prairie planting' is sometimes applied to random plantings of grasses and herbaceous species, but where it is not naturally occurring, it should be considered as a form of ornamental planting.

Prairie planting on an estate in Illinois, USA.

A wildflower meadow in the Bavarian Alps.

Part of a wildflower meadow in Sussex on a thin chalky soil.

Focal-point planting

We can use plants as the focal points for our compositions, but only if they are strong enough visually to stand out from their surroundings. Sometimes there will be a suitable existing tree on site — a large copper beech (*Fagus sylvatica f.* purpurea) would be a good example — in which case I use it as the starting point for a composition, clearing the trunk, creating an axis towards it and perhaps adding some additional planting to enhance the overall picture.

The alternatives to plants as focal points are structures: fountains, openings, seats and statues. These are often easier to use where there are no suitable existing plants, since it takes time for new plants to grow large enough to have the necessary impact. Sometimes I use a seat or statue as the immediate focal point, but then plant a tree behind it, which will eventually replace the seat or statue.

There are several visual qualities found in plants that make them stand out as potential focal points, and these include a strong shape, a defined habit, coarse texture and coloured foliage. Plants with these qualities are often listed as architectural plants and they include:

- *Columnar shape,*
- *Spiky shape,*
- *Cone shape,*
- *Weeping habit,*
- *Horizontal habit,*
- *Large leaves.*

Coloured foliage will also stand out provided that the surrounding foliage is green, and a coloured-leaved architectural plant will have additional impact as a focal point.

Usually focal-point plants are individual specimens, but a group can also work well, for example a group of white-stemmed birch trees is more effective than a single specimen.

Enhancing a focal point

Plants can be used to enhance a focal point; they should be selected for this specific purpose, and need to relate visually to the focal point in both scale and/or visual characteristics. A good example would be a weeping willow (*Salix x sepuchralis* var. *chrycosoma*, syn *S. alba* 'Tristis', or *S. babylonica*) beside a waterfall, or a pair of fan-shaped cherry trees on either side of an opening. More formal examples would be a pair of box balls in pots either side of a formal gateway, or columnar conifers either side of a seat.

Cornus controversa 'Variegata', with its horizontal habit and variegated foliage, makes an effective focal point.

This focal-point gazebo is enhanced by box hedging, an avenue of mophead hollies and staddle stones leading towards it, and more box hedging that provides it with a green base and planters of topiary on either side of the structure.

This wide mixed border has a high hornbeam hedge providing a background in scale with the border.

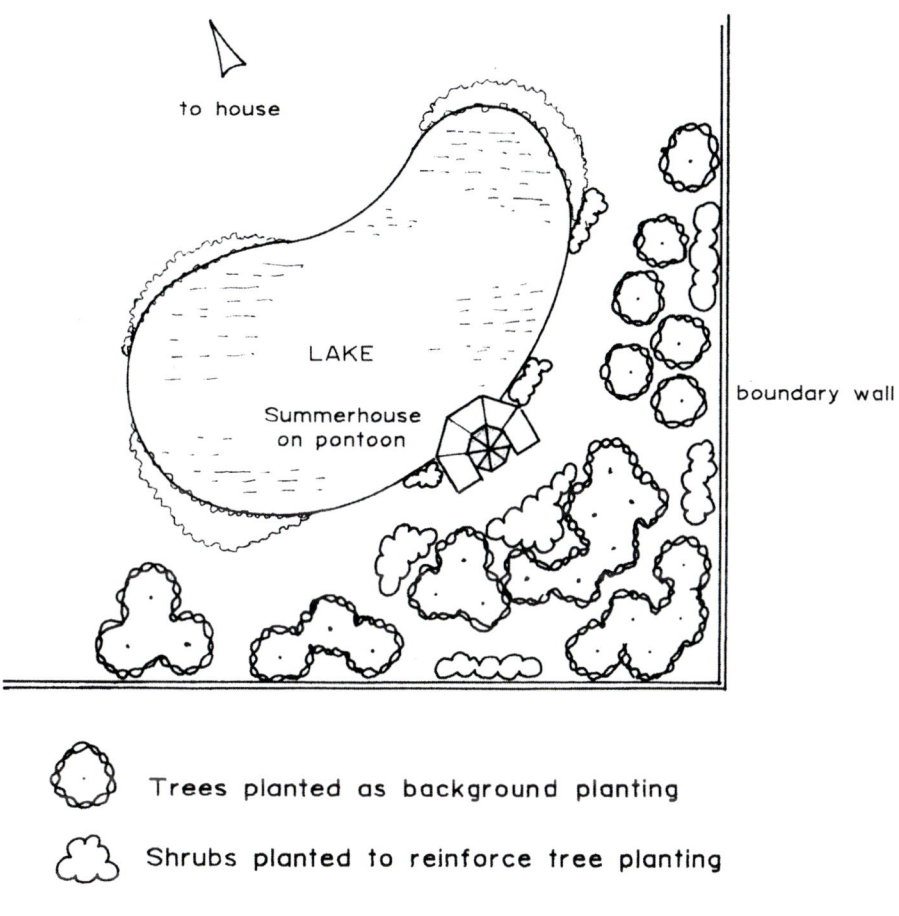

Part of the plan of a large informal garden where trees have been planted beyond a new lake to provide a green background to a summerhouse and pontoon.

Figure 2.3 Planting to provide a background.

Background planting

This is the use of plants to provide a suitable background to a focal point. In a sense it is part of structural planting as it provides vertical lines, but I prefer to consider these plants when I am selecting my focal points. Alternatives would be fences or walls, but planting is often more appropriate, more attractive and cheaper! Alternatively a dramatic backdrop for larger features can be provided by the sky as it changes colour and moods with the weather, the time of day and the season of the year.

Most focal points, though, need to be seen against a plain background which does not detract from the feature itself. Seats need a background which provides a feeling of comfort and privacy. Plants in a border often have more impact when given a dark green background, and here it is important that the background does not conflict with the border itself. The fine texture and dull colour of conifers often provide the best solution.

GROUND-COVER PLANTING 23

Ornamental planting

Ornamental planting is the use of plants to add extra colour or interest to the garden and is usually planted in beds or borders. For many garden owners this is the main reason for having a garden allowing them to indulge in an enjoyable leisure activity. There are, however, many beautiful landscaped gardens in which there is virtually no ornamental planting at all and it is not an essential part of good design.

Ornamental planting needs maintenance; in the case of bedding roses this includes, pruning, feeding, spraying, dead-heading and weeding, a successful herbaceous border needs weeding, staking, feeding, dead-heading, and regular lifting and dividing the plants. So when asked to design a garden for clients who are not gardeners, I make sure that I add colour and seasonal interest to the structural and ground-cover planting without including any areas of specifically ornamental planting. The ground-cover planting will need some weeding in the establishment period but very little attention otherwise.

Clients who do want ornamental planting may want it because they would like to include one or more of the following:

- *Rose bed,*
- *Herbaceous border,*
- *Mixed border,*
- *Seasonal bedding,*
- *Herb garden,*
- *Rock plants,*
- *Water-garden plants,*
- *Climbing plants,*
- *'New Wave' plantings.*

Or they may want to include plants for a specific theme or purpose such as:

- *A cottage garden,*
- *A butterfly garden,*
- *A wildlife garden.*

They may want to include a feature which needs planting to enhance it:

A pergola, trellis or arbour which needs climbing plants;
A pond which needs water and bog plants both to enhance it and to help keep the water clear of algae;
Rocks which need alpines or rock plants;
Ornamental pots which need seasonal bedding or specimen plants.

Clients decide which type of ornamental planting they wish to be included. I find the place for them in my design or, alternatively, once the potential ability to maintain an area of ornamental planting has been established, I may include areas of ornamental planting to add interest to my design: that is, I add some beds and borders. I may then suggest to the client the type of ornamental planting for each of the beds and borders I have included.

There really is no such thing as all-year-round interest when we use ornamental planting. We need to plan for one period of maximum impact with some residual interest at other times of the year. The main seasons for flower borders are early summer, with lupins, peonies and delphiniums; mid to late summer, with roses, phlox, day-lilies, kniphofias; and autumn, with crocosmia, Japanese anemones, michaelmas daisies, chrysanthemums and dahlias. For spring I usually plan mixed borders to include bulbs and spring flowering shrubs, and for winter hellebores with red-stemmed dogwoods and grey junipers.

Before going further it is important to understand that plants may fulfill more than one design objective, for example an avenue of cherry trees will be both structural and ornamental. In this case I select plants for their primary function first, which would be the shape and size of the cherry trees, and then look for good blossom or autumn colour.

Summary

Planting design is the selection and use of plants to achieve the desired design objectives.

There are five ways in which plants can be used in garden design:

1. **Functional planting** – plants which are needed for a purpose, e.g. vegetables, but these plantings will not necessarily form part of the overall design.
   - *Screen planting,*
   - *Wind protection,*
   - *Shade,*
   - *Noise reduction,*
   - *Food plants.*

   This section is covered in Chapter 1 but given here for completeness.

2. **Structural planting** – gives structure and vertical lines and form:
   - *To create the lines of the design;*
   - *To delineate space;*
   - *To reinforce vistas and/or axes.*

3. **Ground-cover planting** – to create horizontal cover and/or pattern, and is;
   - *Formal,*
   - *Informal, or*
   - *Natural.*

4. **Focal-point planting** – to provide focal points for compositions with:
   - *Specimen trees or shrubs* used as a focal point;
   - *Planting to frame or enhance* a focal point;
   - *Background planting.*

5. **Ornamental planting** – to provide colour and seasonal interest with:
   - *Beds and borders;*
   - *Planting to enhance a feature,* e.g. water plants.

All plants placed in a garden or landscape should be selected for one of these five categories of plant use, if not they will look out of place and good design is compromised. I have already stated, but it is worth repeating that, as a designer, you should know the purpose of every single plant you include in your designs.

This path has plants on either side; others form an arch of dappled shade above to entice the visitor to explore further.

This was an old border which was large and difficult to maintain, so I divided it into two smaller borders with a wide grass path in the centre and reduced the width by adding a grass path at the back. An elderly mulberry tree provides an effective focal point and a background of trees screen the buildings behind.

3 PLANNING PLANTED AREAS

Factors to be considered

While still at the overall design stage, you will need to decide on the size, shape, position and number of planted areas to be included, and then make sure that each area is of an appropriate size for the type of planting you wish to include, and that it will fulfill the design criteria you have assigned to it. Factors you may need to consider include:

a) The size of the house and garden

As already mentioned, in any design project you must always be aware of the scale you are dealing with, and be sure that all the elements are in proportion to this scale; this also includes the sizes of planted areas. So a large house and garden requires larger lawns and more generous planted areas, and a small town garden may need a smaller grass area and relatively small beds and borders. Hopefully the outside space is in proportion to the house, but it is not always so, and if not, you have to decide how to cope with the different scales. A small cottage with a large country garden, for example, may benefit from having the garden divided into areas, so that near the house the smaller proportions of a cottage garden still work.

b) The style of the house and garden

Formal houses respond to formal gardens, rambling country houses to a more informal approach. However, the client may well prefer a particular style, and this has to overrule any other factors. Formal gardens need formally shaped beds and symmetry, whether bilateral or quadrilateral. Country gardens often work well with informal lawns and curving beds and borders. Town gardens may need to be designed using formal shapes arranged asymmetrically, and the gardens of modern blocks of flats or hotels may respond to an abstract design.

c) Types of plants to be included

The plants chosen may dictate the shape of bed in which they are to be planted. Bedding roses look attractive when planned in a formal arrangement of formal shapes, whereas a mixed shrub border often looks more natural in an informal shape and setting. Herbs have traditionally been planted in formal beds, but I have seen them planted very attractively in an informal border. A wildflower meadow by its very nature needs to be informal, as do most of the more naturalistic types of planting.

d) Maintenance available

If there is to be little or no maintenance, then planning lots of complicated planting areas is totally inappropriate unless they are to be filled with a single species of plant like ivy. On the other hand, if there is a team of gardeners available, you can have a whole range of different planted areas. Really keen owners are almost better than a team of gardeners because they can work much longer hours and at weekends.

Sizes of planted areas

Functional planting

I usually work out the size of planted areas to be used for functional planting right from the beginning of the planning stage. Taking each type of functional planting I work within the following dimensions:

Screen planting – whether the screen is needed on the boundaries, to hide unwanted views, to give privacy or for protection from wind, the following widths of planting can be used depending on the space you have available:

Widths for screen planting

- 300mm – Fence with trellis on top and row of climbers.
- 600mm – Fence with narrow hedge – a 'fedge'.
  Pleached trees.
- 800mm – Clipped hedge, e.g. *Fagus sylvatica*.
- 900mm – Clipped coniferous hedge.
- 1200mm – Informal hedge, native hedge.
- 1500mm – Row of conifers; but they will need some clipping in later years.

> **Shelter belts** — these need at least:
>
> 9000mm — For two rows trees planted at 3000mm centres and a row of shrubs on the garden side.
>
> 10000mm — For three rows trees planted at 3000mm centres.

You can see examples of shelter belts planted along many of our roads, where the trees are only 2000mm apart; to me this would seem an unnecessary waste of trees.

Noise reduction — You need a dense hedge or row of conifers for successful noise reduction, and the wider the planting the better. If the hedge is to be planted on top of a bank, allow at least 3000mm for the base of the bank.

Houses screened using a row of pleached limes, which are planted 900mm in from the boundary fence to allow space for a hornbeam hedge.

A shelter belt to an arboretum in Dorset; the trees in the belt are planted 3000mm apart, and with a third row of trees placed 9000mm in from the boundary fence.

28 PLANNING PLANTED AREAS

Food plants

The space needed for food production will depend on the client's wishes and the amount of maintenance available. The client may ask for fruit trees, soft fruit and vegetables; all need good soil and sunshine for most, if not all, of the day.

Fruit — fruit trees, such as apples, pears, plums and cherries, need to have full sun on all their branches to ripen their fruit. A traditional orchard layout is based on standard trees planted at 8000mm x 8000mm apart, which means an area of 24m x 32m is needed for an orchard of 12 standard trees. Today many clients are happier with half standard trees, which fruit at an earlier age and are easier to harvest. These still need 5000mm x 5000mm spacing so our 12 trees need 15m x 20m. There are bush trees available which can be planted 4000mm apart, but these are far less attractive than half standard trees, so usually I do not suggest them. Where there is little room, I promote the idea of a row of cordon fruit, which I will often use to screen the vegetable garden. Cordons are planted 800mm to 900mmm apart and supported on wires strained between posts. An alternative is espalier or fan-trained fruit trees which can be grown on wires and posts or against a wall, and will need to be spaced at 4000mm apart.

Soft fruit usually require a cage to protect the ripening fruit from birds. These can be ornamental but the basic fruit cage is fairly unattractive and usually needs screening. Soft bush fruits including redcurrants, blackcurrants and gooseberries are planted 1500mm apart and raspberry canes planted in rows 450mm apart within the rows, and adjacent rows 1500mm apart to allow access for picking. As a guide, a 6000mm x 6000mm fruit cage will allow for 8 bush fruits and 2 rows of raspberries.

Vegetables need to be in full sun, and I now usually plant them on raised beds 1200mm wide with 600mm paths between, which allows for cultivating the beds without walking on them. Traditionally vegetables were grown on a three-year rotation system to reduce pest and disease problems: the first year would be root vegetables, the next brassicas, and the third year other vegetables and salad crops. Many of my clients still want to be able to follow this system, so at least three beds are needed, plus an extra bed if they want to include potatoes. These can be arranged in parrallel rows, or more decoratively as a potager. A potager is a formal vegetable garden often arranged with quadrilateral symmetry, and with box hedges around each bed. This then becomes less functional and more ornamental, and may not need screening.

A row of cordon apple trees screening the vegetable garden.

Structural planting

As I begin to work on the shapes and lines of my designs, so I start thinking about how these are going to be created. I may use walls, fences, pergolas or plants. Frequently the lines are created by hedges and avenues, and I use the widths below as a guide.

Hedges are frequently used in structural planting, and you need to decide on the final width of the hedge as you place it on the plan. The plants will then be placed in the centre of this distance.

Width of hedges

300-500mm	Dwarf hedge kept clipped e.g. *Buxus sempervirens*.
600-800mm	Deciduous hedge kept clipped e.g. *Fagus sylvatica*.
900mm	Clipped coniferous hedge.
1200mm	Informal hedge, native hedge.

Ensure that there is enough room to allow the hedge to grow out and then be cut on both sides.

Most hedges are planted in single rows of plants, but for a denser hedge both hornbeam (*Carpinus betulus*) and beech (*Fagus sylvatica*) are planted in double rows with 450mm between plants and 300mm between rows.

The recently planted box hedges surrounding beds of herbs are to be kept clipped at 400mm wide; the mature yew hedges are regularly hard-pruned to maintain a 1000mm width.

Native hedges are often a planning condition for boundary planting and look more appropriate for gardens within the countryside. The shrubs used vary in different parts of Britain depending on the soil, climate and local practice. In the past they usually comprised a single species, commonly hawthorn (*Crataegus monogyna*) which provides a dense stock-proof hedge, but in some areas beech (*Fagus sylvatica*) or hornbeam (*Carpinus betulus*) were planted. Over the years these hedges became mixed when seeds of other plants drifted in with the wind or were carried by birds and small mammals. Mixed native hedges are now usually planted because they give a greater range of nesting sites, protection and food for native fauna.

An informal hedge of Rosa rugosa *surrounding a tennis court; planted eight years previously with an intended minimum width of 1200mm which it has been allowed to exceed.*

A hedge of native plants in northern Illinois where the client wanted an English landscape including hedges of mixed shrubs.

Native hedge species

The following plants are included in mixed hedging but should only be included if ecologically correct for the area being planted.

Acer campestre	— field maple,
Cornus sanguinea	— dogwood,
Corylus avellana	— hazel,
Crataegus monogyna	— hawthorn,
Euonymus europaeus	— spindle,
Prunus spinosa	— sloe,
Salix caprea	— goat willow,
Sambucus nigra	— elder,
Viburnum lantana	— wayfaring tree,
Viburnum opulus	— guelder-rose.

For a chalk soil the mixture might be

5 no. *Crataegus monogyna*
3 no. *Cornus sanguinea*
3 no. *Acer campestre*
2 no. *Euonymus europaeus*
1 no. *Corylus avellana*

Plant two parallel rows of plants with 300mm between the rows and with plants in the rows 450mm apart.

An avenue of cherry trees leads the eye towards the view of the church spire in the distance.

more in scale with the drive to a cottage, and an avenue of horse chestnut trees would be more appropriate for the drive to a manor house. Avenues are most effective when planted with all trees of the same species. I plant the trees as a series of squares so that the distance between trees is the same both across and up the drive.

Avenues consist of two rows of trees or shrubs planted parallel to each other and frequently planted either side of a drive or path to add impact. Clients may want an avenue to enhance their drive, or as designer you may wish to add an avenue to enhance a vista or to create light and shade; nevertheless an avenue should always lead somewhere. When selecting trees for an avenue, take care to keep the ultimate size of the trees in proportion with the width of the drive and the size of the building to which it leads. For example, an avenue of apple trees would be

Trees which make attractive avenues

Species	Ultimate Height	Ultimate Spread	Planting Distance
Small trees			
Amelanchier arborea 'Robin Hill'	6m	5m	5m
Crataegus laevigata 'Paul's Scarlet'	6m	6m	5m
Crataegus persimilis 'Prunifolia'	8m	6m	5m
Prunus 'Pink Perfection'	8m	8m	6m
Pyrus calleryana 'Chanticleer'	10m	5m	5m
Sorbus 'Joseph Rock'	10m	5m	5m
Medium Trees			
Carpinus betulus 'Fastigiata'	15m	5m	8m
Prunus avium 'Plena'	15m	12m	8m
Sorbus aria 'Lutescens'	12m	8m	8m
Large Trees			
Castanea sativa	18m	12m	12m
Fagus sylvatica	25m	16m	12m
Platanus x hispanica	20m	12m	12m
Tilia cordata 'Greenspire'	20m	10m	12m

Ground-cover planting

At this stage the areas which will be grass are shown on the plan, including both mown and longer grass areas. Depending on the space available, the longer grass may need mown paths to give access to enjoy any planting within it; the path needs to be the cutting width of the mower to be used or multiples of it. I usually plant bulbs for naturalizing in long grass areas and, if the area is large enough, I include some specimen shrubs and trees for added seasonal interest. Specimen shrubs need 2000mm of space for growth, and plenty of space left between adjacent shrubs.

Any areas which are not practical for growing grass, due to the topography or shade, need to be addressed and decisions made as to whether these areas should be planted with a single species, for example Ivy (*Hedera helix*), or drifts of two or three different species.

Natural ground-cover areas have no size restrictions, but consideration will need to be given to maintenance; for instance, I usually include 4500mm wide bark paths in woodland areas.

If clients have requested parterres or knot gardens, they need to be placed on the plan allowing sufficient room to create the required pattern. I find that an area 5000mm x 5000mm allows plenty of room for a creative design.

Focal-point planting

The amount of room for focal points depends on what is chosen, and then whether it needs planting to enhance it or to provide a background. A background hedge will require the spacing listed above. Planting to enhance may be a planted pot placed either side or possibly beds or borders, but space needs to be left for whatever is needed.

An unmowable bank planted with Pachysandra terminalis.

Ornamental planting

Finally, having allocated sufficient space to all the functional, structural, ground-cover and focal-point planting, I consider the ornamental planting which needs to be included, deciding on whether they will be in beds or borders.

Beds versus borders — I tend to use the terms beds and borders indiscriminately for planted areas, but in fact they are different. A bed has no background and can be accessed and viewed all round, whereas a border is one-sided and set against a hedge, wall or fence so that it is usually viewed from the front and sometimes, but not always, from the side. Beds need space for small plants along all edges and taller plants in the middle, unless planted with a range of varieties of the same or similar heights. A border generally has lower plants at the front and sides, rising to the tallest plants at the back. However, that is not always the case for there is a vogue for looking through taller plants to lower plants beyond which, in my experience, is fine if it works, but a complete mess if it does not.

At this stage it is important to ensure that any areas shown as beds or borders are capable of being planted effectively. With too narrow a border, there will not be room for more than a row of climbing plants, so if you were planning a rose bed for that space it will be impossible. It is very easy during the design process to put in narrow borders without checking their width, particularly in small gardens. Any borders less than 600mm wide should always be planted with a single species, such as *Alchemilla mollis*. A mixture of plants just looks untidy, and beds less than 1200mm wide need the same treatment.

A narrow border 450mm wide planted with a row of Alchemilla mollis. *The clematis trained along the wall behind is planted in an adjacent border.*

The following widths give an indication of the potential planting for beds and borders:

300mm — trained climbing plant or a clipped dwarf hedge.
450mm — trained climbing plant plus dwarf hedge or single row of ground-cover plants.
600mm — trained climbing plant plus row of ground-cover plants or clipped hedge.
900mm — row of small roses and edging plant or clipped hedge.
1200mm — wall shrub plus single row herbaceous; minimum size for a bed.
1500mm — climber plus 2 or 3 rows herbaceous; a bed will have room for an edging at 450mm plus a row of herbaceous plants or bedding roses in the middle.
1800mm — minimum size for an herbaceous border; a bed can have four rows of plants at 450mm spacing.
2400mm — minimum size for a mixed border; good size for a rose bed.
3000mm — a good size for herbaceous border; minimum size for shrub border.
3600mm — a good size for mixed border or bed.
Over 6000mm a bed or border becomes too wide for easy maintenance so, where possible, divide up the area with a path

A border 1100mm wide planted with a row of Rosa 'Summer Dreams' and an edging of box. (below left)

A formal border along the house, which is planted to be seen from both the garden and inside the house. The width is 1500mm. (below right)

If the planted area is planned as a border, it may need to have a background; if so; there needs to be room left for this at the planning stage. A fence takes almost no room at all, but a wall needs a minimum of 225mm width, and a hedge 600mm. A hedge will also need trimming, and it is always sensible to allow a minimum of 450mm for a path between the hedge and the back of a border to allow for hedge growth, access for trimming, and to reduce competition for food and water between hedge and border plants. In large borders there may be room for a background of shrubs; I would then leave a 450mm space between shrubs and the border again to allow access for maintenance.

The next stage will be to select the plants for each area but, first, it is important to understand the visual qualities of different plants and the importance of this in placing plants together.

A 4000mm-wide mixed border backed by a mature hedge and which allows room for large clumps of herbaceous plants plus shrubs chosen for their shape or foliage colour.

An informal border 3000mm wide with a background of small trees.

4 THE VISUAL QUALITIES OF PLANTS 1 — SHAPE, HABIT AND TEXTURE

Designers need to know the shape, habit, texture, colour and size of each plant they wish to use in order to design really well. In design terms, these qualities become important when they are clearly discernible in the individual plant, so that it can contribute to the overall design.

The **shape** of a plant is its outline when seen as a silhouette. This is most clearly seen in deciduous plants during the summer, but all the year round with evergreens. A range of different shapes can be seen in plant outlines from the smaller scale of an individual leaf, to a flower, flower inflorescence, fruit or fruit cluster.

The **habit** of a plant is the direction in which its stems, branches, leaves or flowers grow. In deciduous trees and shrubs the habit is most obvious in winter, but in some plants, such as many conifers, the foliage covers the branches all year; the habit is never visible and is therefore unimportant.

Plant **texture** is the surface pattern created by the shape and arrangement of its leaves. Interesting textures are also found in some stems and some larger flowers and fruit.

Colour in plants usually refers to flower colour, but to the planting designer the colour of foliage is often much more important. In considering foliage colour, it is the subtle differences between the various shades of green which are as important as the dramatic purple, yellow and variegated leaf colours which can be seen in some plants.

The **size** of the whole plant, and of individual parts of plants, will also affect how a particular plant is to be used in designs.

When selecting plants, the most important visual quality depends on how the plant is to be used in the overall design. In structural planting, the size, shape and texture may be more important, whereas when a plant is to be used as a focal point, its shape, habit or colour will influence the choice. In ornamental planting, texture and flower colour may be the deciding features.

Shape

Some designers use the term 'form' instead of 'shape', but I prefer to use shape because form can be confused with 'habit'. For instance, one might use the term 'weeping form' for a willow when, in fact, it is the weeping habit of its branches that is seen, and the outline shape of the tree may be round or dome-shaped.

As already stated, the shape of a plant, leaf or flower is only important if it can be clearly defined and is large enough to create an impact from where it is viewed. When one looks at a group of trees from a distance, the shapes of leaves and flowers will only be seen as part of the texture; but close up in a border, the round shape of, say, a bergenia leaf or peony flower will produce a more dramatic impact.

There are ten different and distinct shapes that can be seen in trees, shrubs and conifers, and a further three which are visually important in flowers.

Round or ***spherical shapes*** are those where the plant forms a ball with equal height and width, and with the base curving in. In trees it is the round shape which is supported by the trunk, whereas in shrubs and herbaceous plants there is no trunk and the shape sits on the ground. Round shapes are formal and geometric, and tend to draw the eye towards them, so that they need to be used with some care. Round trees make good formal avenues and minor focal points. Clipped balls add formality to any area and in pairs can be used on either side of a focal point or, to add dramatic emphasis, spaced regularly along an informally planted bed or border.

Round shapes are also effective when used together with other circular features such as stone balls. They also work well with other geometric shapes including cones and squares.

Round shapes can be found in many leaves and are often seen as part of a rounded texture rather than individually.

Round shapes in flowers can be seen in single flowers, such as in *Paeonia officinalis*, or in the floral inflorescence of *Allium* 'Purple Splendour'. A range of rounded flowers included within an individual border can be very effective.

Dome shapes can be seen in a wide range of plants, including many of the low-growing ones which form 'hummocks'. Dome-shaped plants have rounded tops, with their width greater than their height. They are useful shapes in planting design because they relate readily to the wider landscape: for example, in Britain where many hills have rounded tops.

Low domes planted at the base of buildings act as effective visual anchors, and dome-shaped trees make attractive informal avenues, or create a soft arching effect when planted on each side of a gateway

Bell shapes are another rounded form, but this time with the height greater than the width and the base spread outwards. This shape is often seen in weeping trees and in many larger, British native trees. Bells are gentle shapes, and a mass of bell shapes together provide effective background planting; a row of bell-shaped shrubs can create an attractive informal hedge. There are many bell-shaped leaves and flowers, but the actual visual impact of the shape depends on the habit of the leaf or flower. The pendulous bell-shaped flowers of *Campanula punctata*, for example, have a different visual effect compared with the upright bells of *Campanula trachelium*.

All three rounded shapes work well together and, in mixed planting, bell and dome shapes can reduce the formal effect of round balls.

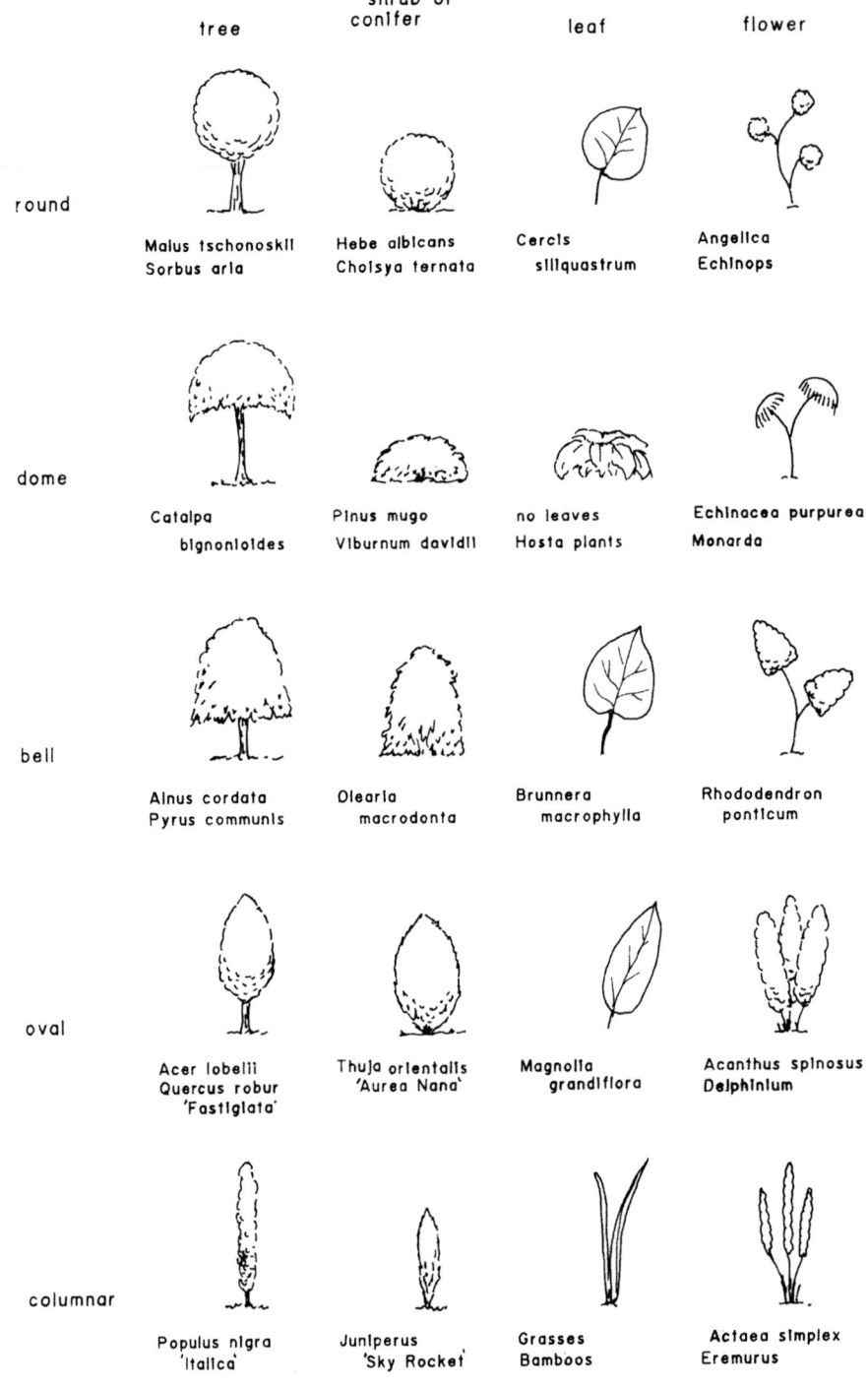

Figure 4.1 Shapes found in plants: round to columnar.

A tree clipped into a round shape.

The round flowers of Angelica archangelica *and* Viburnum opulus *harmonize with each other.*

A dome-shaped tree.

The **oval** is a more formal shape with the width of the plant being less than half the overall height. The top and base can be straight, in which case the shape is more cylindrical. In the true oval, both top and base curve inwards. Nurseries have selected plants with this shape, and the cultivar name 'Erecta' usually indicates an oval or cylindrical shape. This is a very useful shape in design because it gives height to a landscape, and acts as a foil for horizontal planting. Oval-shaped shrubs are useful for tall hedging.

The majority of leaves have an oval shape, which contributes to a generally rounded texture, except where the leaves are large enough to have an individual impact as in *Magnolia grandiflora*.

The shape is **columnar** when the width is much less than the height. This is an extreme shape and, if wrongly placed, becomes a visual eyesore: it will stick out like the proverbial 'sore thumb'. Columnar shapes are best treated as green pillars and used in pairs, lines, squares or circles. They will always form focal points when placed on their own, and this effect will only work visually when placed with great care as one would with an obelisk.

There are many columnar leaves, most specifically amongst all the monocots. They contribute to a linear texture. Columnar flower or flower inflorescences are very dramatic when seen individually, as with

The bell-shaped flowers of Digitalis purpurea.

The strong oval shape of Taxus baccata *'Fastigiata'.*

Columnar-shaped conifers.

The columnar spikes of Chamerion angustifolium 'Album'.

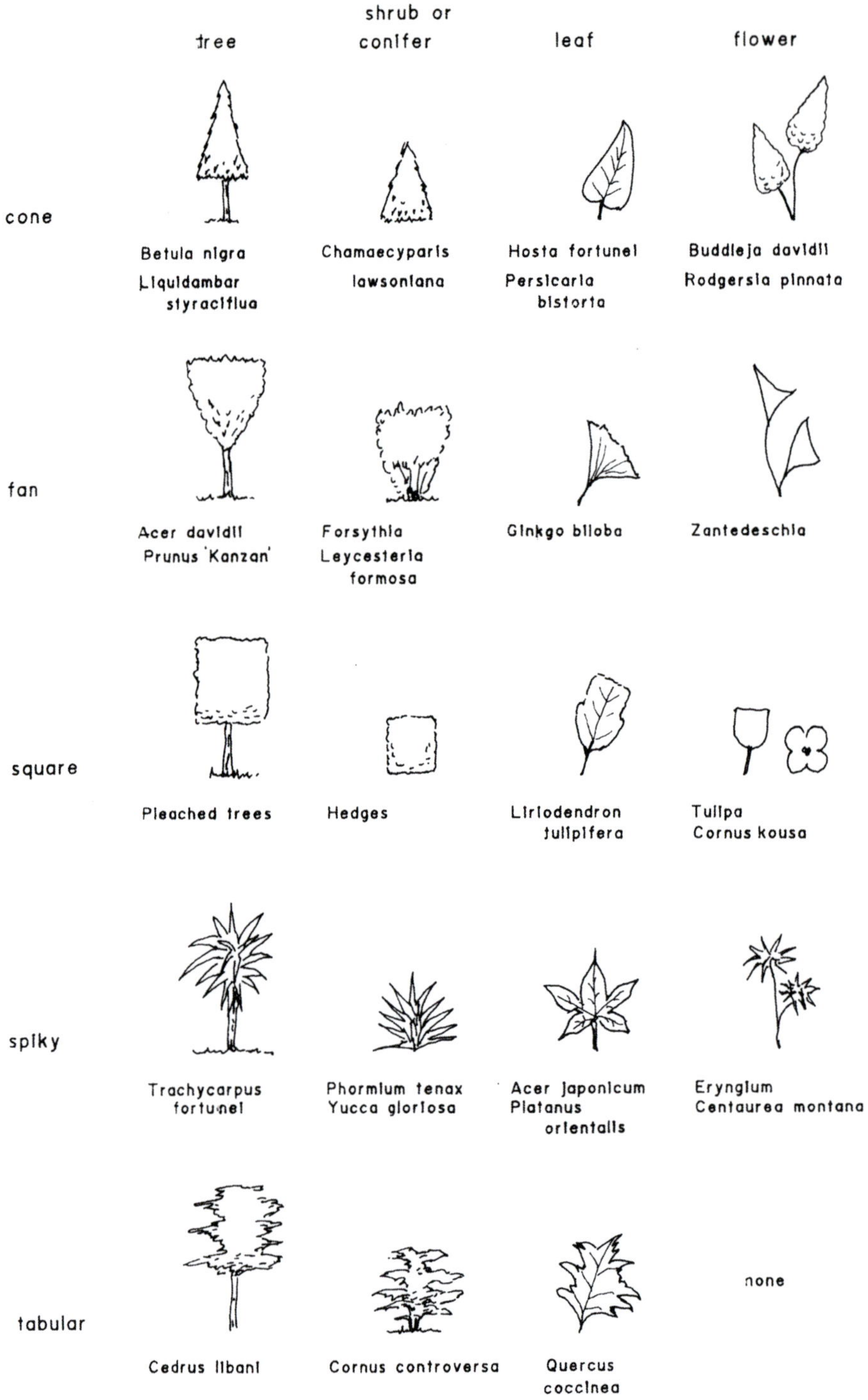

	tree	shrub or conifer	leaf	flower
cone	Betula nigra, Liquidambar styraciflua	Chamaecyparis lawsoniana	Hosta fortunei, Persicaria bistorta	Buddleja davidii, Rodgersia pinnata
fan	Acer davidii, Prunus 'Kanzan'	Forsythia, Leycesteria formosa	Ginkgo biloba	Zantedeschia
square	Pleached trees	Hedges	Liriodendron tulipifera	Tulipa, Cornus kousa
spiky	Trachycarpus fortunei	Phormium tenax, Yucca gloriosa	Acer japonicum, Platanus orientalis	Eryngium, Centaurea montana
tabular	Cedrus libani	Cornus controversa	Quercus coccinea	none

Figure 4.2 *Shapes found in plants: cone to tabular.*

Eremurus bungeii, and can give added emphasis to a border particularly when repeated along its length.

The **cone** shape is a natural form in younger landscapes where volcanoes or unweathered mountains appear, such as in the Rocky Mountains of the USA and Canada. A cone has a pointed top and wide base. It is characteristic of many conifers and in some young trees where the leader is growing more quickly than the side branches. It is not seen as a shape in shrubs or herbaceous plants, but can be found in some leaves and flowers.

Use cones in groups or as focal points, and for formal avenues and as corners of formal beds.

The **fan** shape is an inverted cone, seen mostly in shrubs with several upright stems which fan out at the top. It is not very important in design terms except in fan-shaped trees which can be used as focal points or as a pair placed to frame a view.

The **square** shape is not found in nature but is frequently created by humans in the form of trimmed hedges, pleached trees and individual clipped cubes. It is a very formal shape, and can look out of place in all but the most formal of areas. When used well, the shape gives very strong lines to a design. It has been seen more recently in 'green walls'

Box clipped into a formal cone shape.

Yew clipped into an oblong.

added to buildings, although this idea was widely used in French gardens as 'fedges' with a hedge planted in front of a wall or fence. The square shape is found in a few flowers and one or two leaves.

A **spiky** outline has a series of points, and is a very strong shape which is naturally found in arid environments. In more temperate areas, the spiky shape can look out of place and create an instant focal point. Such shapes can upset the balance of a mixed border unless placed very carefully. They are often seen at their best in gravel gardens where the whole shape can be appreciated. Spiky-leaf shapes are found in many of the maples and contribute to an overall angular texture.

The **tabular** shape is often found in trees and shrubs with a horizontal habit; It is usually quite dramatic and makes an instant focal point, either on its own or seen against the backdrop of buildings.

The spiky shape of a yucca.

Saucer-shaped flowers of Campanula persicifolia.

Square flowers.

Round fruits of Rosa rugosa.

Flower shapes

There are several specific shapes which are found in flowers and these include:

- **Daisy** — this is found in the flowers of the plants belonging to the family *Asteraceae*, and harmonizes well with the linear texture of grasses.

- **Saucer** — the saucer can be considered as a shallow bell or upside-down dome, and is found in a range of flowers including those belonging to the *Ranunculaceae*, *Campanulaceae* and *Rosaceae* families. It harmonizes with all the round shapes

- **Fleur-de-lis** is a very strong shape seen most strikingly in irises, but also found in other plants including aquilegia. Use it in borders but be sure to repeat it along the length of the bed.

Fruit shape can be important when the fruits are large enough to have a visual impact. Round and cone-shaped fruit, and uniquely pods and winged fruits, can be included in a design, though the last two are probably not significant visually.

The daisy-shaped flowers of osteospermum.

The fleur-de-lis shape of the iris flower.

The fleur-de-lis shape of the aquilegia flower.

Habit

Habit, as previously mentioned, is the direction in which a plant grows, and this description can apply to stems, branches, leaf stems and flowers. It is only important as a visual quality when it is clearly seen, and for most deciduous plants this will be in winter rather than during the rest of the year. Some habits are so dramatic that they are important all year round, for example in weeping willows where the main stems are weeping and the leaves are pendulous, thus adding to the overall effect. If you have to struggle to decide the habit of a plant, it follows that it does not have an important visual quality; thus, it does not need to be considered when using it in planting design.

There are seven habits exhibited by plants which I consider to be important in planting design.

Weeping

A weeping habit is only found in trees and is seen when all the main branches hang down from the central trunk. It is always very striking, and weeping trees make good focal points particularly in association with water; falling water echoes the fall of the branches. A weeping habit can be found with round, dome, bell, or oval shapes. All of them make focal points, but weeping, oval-shaped trees

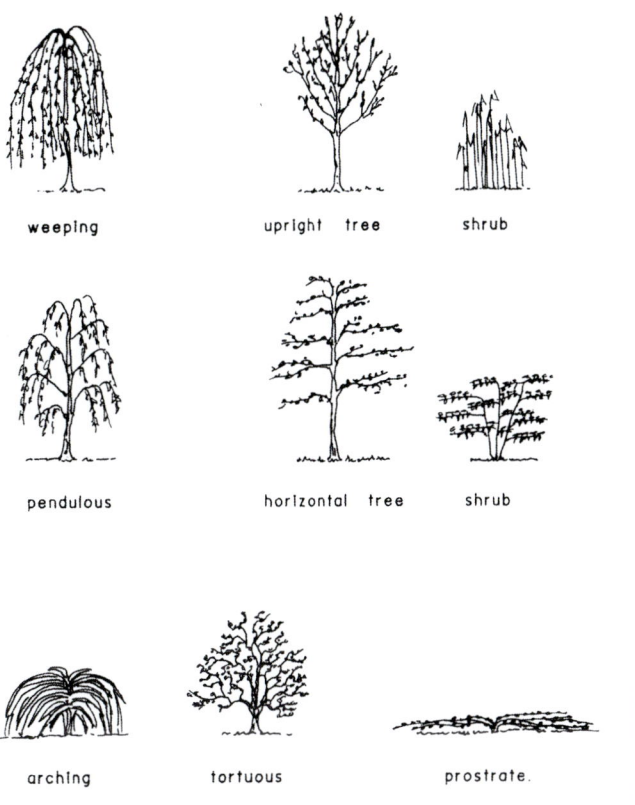

Figure 4.3 *Habits of plants.*

The pendulous habit of the weeping willow frequently seen as its most attractive planted next to water.

The weeping habits of Salix 'Kilmarnock', which is even more dramatic in winter.

HABIT 43

are better placed in pairs rather than individually because they tend to stand out like 'sore thumbs'.

Pendulous

Trees and shrubs with a pendulous habit have upright branches with drooping ends, and both leaves and flowers can also be pendulous. This habit is visually softer than weeping, and using pendulous plants together can create a beautiful effect. Nevertheless a group of pendulous trees can seem rather sombre if planted too closely, but look less gloomy when spaced out more generously along an avenue or planted individually adjacent to a building.

Many flowers and some leaves have a pendulous habit but the overall effect will usually depend on the habit of the branches and stems.

Arching

An arching habit is found in the stems of shrubs and in the leaves of many herbaceous plants. The effect of arching is more pronounced where the leaves are linear, as with many of the grasses. It is a lovely habit and adds softness to planting schemes. An arching habit can look particularly effective when the overall shape of the plant is a dome. Such plants make a very effective base planting around walls and buildings.

A large number of shrubs have arching habits, and these plants can look particularly effective when the ground around is left bare, or covered in low ground-cover plants to allow the habit to be appreciated. Many arching shrubs look much more effective when regularly pruned to remove any non-branching stems, and to thin the centre of the shrub.

Upright

Important examples of completely vertical habits are the stems of bamboos or the coloured stems of dogwoods in winter. The vertical habit in leaves is most dramatic when they are large or fleshy, as with yuccas and phormiums. In these species the upright habit helps to create the spiky shapes which, as already mentioned, need to be placed with great care because such plants always make focal points unless positioned amidst plants with a similar shape and habit.

Arching habits.

The upright habit of a red-stemmed bamboo making a dramatic statement in a park in Kuala Lumpur.

Many stems of flower inflorescences are upright, as with delphiniums, lupins and verbascums. The vertical line found in such plants can be used to add height and drama to a border, particularly when similar plants are repeated along the length of the planting.

Horizontal

This is a very dramatic habit where the branches start growing vertically, but then spread out horizontally and create a 'horizontal line', thereby leading to a tabular shape. It may take many years before the horizontal line is seen in trees such as *Cedrus libani* or *Pinus sylvestris*, but once the horizontal line appears, these trees make very dramatic focal points. Existing mature plants displaying this habit should be used as such. *Cornus controversa* and *Viburnum plicatum* 'Mariesii' can be planted for a more instant result because their 'horizontal line' becomes evident at a much younger age. The term 'horizontal' is also applied to shrubs and conifers with horizontal branches at ground level; however, this gives a very different visual effect and I have included them under prostrate habit below.

Tortuous

A tortuous habit is where the branches are twisted. This occurs in some plants as they mature, but is also found in a few others which have been selected in the nursery for this

The horizontal habit of Viburnum plicatum *'Mariesii'*.

habit. They can be recognized by the cultivar names 'Tortuosa' or 'Contorta'. It is difficult to place tortuous plants because they tend to 'quarrel' visually with other plants and really need to be placed on their own. However, they make exciting focal points when placed by water, rocks or man-made features such as grottoes and arches. Again, some plants will eventually display this habit as they mature, and can then be effectively seen as 'living sculpture' and used as focal points with the stems exposed, and with gravel or low ground-cover planting.

The contorted trunks of a mature rhododendron.

Prostrate

This is where the branches spread out over the ground rather than growing upward so that the plant appears completely flat. A similar effect is often created when climbing plants are planted without support. These plants are useful ground cover where mown grass is not appropriate.

Habits of leaves and flowers

There is one habit specific to leaves that might be used in planting design. This is **rosette** where the leaves form a circle. This habit is visually complementary to round shapes and a rounded texture.

Flower inflorescences often display two habits, and it is their combination that creates different visual effects. An upright stem may have upright or pendulous flowers; the double upright being more formal than the combination of two different habits.

The prostrate habit of Cotoneaster dammeri.

The elegant unfurling habit of ferns in spring.

Black rosettes of Aeonium 'Zwartkop'.

The arching leaves and pendulous flowers of Dierama pulcherrimum *makes it an instant focal point.*

Using shape and habit in planting design

I have already indicated how plants of different shapes and habits can be used in planting plans, but the most important points to remember are:

- Shape and habit are only important if they can be very clearly seen;
- Plants with the same shape or habit harmonize and can be used together;
- Other materials or features with the same shape or habit as a plant will harmonize and can be used together.

Texture

All materials used in design have their own surface patterns or textures. These will range from the fine texture of a gravel path, the shiny surface of a still pool or the coarse texture of the leaves of *Gunnera manicata*. The texture of plants is usually seen as the surface pattern of their leaves, but with some others, such as *Arbutus andrachnoides*, it is the texture of the peeling stems that gives most impact. The texture of flowers is only significant when larger-flowered plants are used in an herbaceous or mixed border.

Two different textures can be seen in the leaves of a single plant, where there is the macro-texture of the mass of leaves, but also the micro-texture on the surface of individual leaves. The designer needs to decide which is most important visually. With small-leaved plants the macro texture is usually most important, but with large-leaved plants like gunnera the surface texture can be equally important.

Leaf texture is really much more important than flower texture when grouping plants, because it is seen all year round with evergreens, and throughout the growing season with deciduous plants.

Most books, if they cover texture at all, limit themselves to fine, medium and coarse textures dependent on the size of individual leaves. This approach is far too simplistic: there are many other factors that influence a consideration of texture and may therefore affect the use of a particular plant in a design.

The fine texture of coniferous foliage.

The medium texture of epimedium leaves.

The bold texture of Rodgersia podophylla.

The coarse texture of Petasites japonicus.

The various factors which affect texture are:

Size of leaf,
Shape of leaf,
Surface features, and
Leaf margin.

Size of leaf is usually the dominant factor in considerations of texture. It helps to assign plants into one of the following groups:

Size of leaf

Small	fine texture	e.g., *Erica carnea*
Medium	medium texture	e.g., *Fagus sylvatica*
Large	bold texture	e.g., *Hosta sieboldiana*
Very large	coarse texture	e.g., *Rheum palmatum*

Fine textures are useful in creating peaceful spaces. A mown lawn with beds of fine-leaved heathers and conifers behind is very relaxing although verging on the boring. Conifers with a fine texture also make good hedges behind borders and as background to other features.

Medium textures are useful for general planting and provide a good basis when other visual qualities are important such as shape or habit.

Bold and coarse textures, such as in a clump of rheum beside a pond, can add drama by drawing the eye towards it.

Shape of leaf

I have mentioned this above when discussing shape, but it is worth repeating it here for easy reference:

Leaf Shapes

Round shape	rounded texture	e.g., *Bergenia cordifolia*
Columnar shape	linear texture	e.g., all grasses
Spiky shape	angular texture	e.g., *Acer platanoides*

Surface features

Waxy cuticle	glossy texture	e.g., *Magnolia grandiflora*
Hairs – short	velvety texture	e.g., *Salvia officinalis*
– medium	furry texture	e.g., *Stachys byzantina*
Prickles	prickly texture	e.g., *Ilex aquifolium*
Strong veins	veined texture	e.g., *Viburnum davidii*

Leaf margins

Dissected	dissected texture	e.g., *Acer palmatum* var. *dissectum*
Serrated	serrated texture	e.g., *Melianthus major*

For some plants, particularly those with small leaves, it can be sufficient to use a single word for the texture, for example, **fine**. With plants with larger leaves it may be more appropriate to use two words, such as **medium, shiny texture**. With a few plants it may be necessary to use three words or more: **large, angular, hairy texture**.

There is a whole list of other words used to describe texture including, **feathery, ferny, leathery, scaly, fleshy** and **corrugated**, but it is easier to keep to clearly defined categories rather than trying to decide whether, for example, leathery means 'patent leather' as in *Prunus laurocerasus*, or like old cow hide as in *Viburnum rhytidophyllum*: both have been described as leathery but they are visually poles apart.

Using texture in design

Unlike shape and habit, texture is always apparent and needs to be considered in all planting schemes;

As with shape and habit, plants within the same texture always look good together — the use of plants with a similar texture will provide a calm base to planting design;

Look for similar textures in both hard- and soft-landscaping materials because similar textures in all materials will harmonize.

Prickly texture.

The shiny texture of Magnolia grandifolia.

The corrugated texture of Viburnum rhytidophyllum.

A simple and effective planting of Iris sibirica *and* Geranium macrorrhizum *both of which have arching leaves but very different leaf shapes.*

5 THE VISUAL QUALITIES OF PLANTS 2 — COLOUR AND SIZE

I have discussed the subjects of shape, habit and texture before colour, because in many landscape designs those qualities are much more important plant attributes than colour itself. This is due to the fact that, for much of the time, landscape designers are working with just green in their plant palette.

It is within the specific context of garden design that colour becomes more important. Flowers in their wide range of colours frequently play an important part in a design, and foliage colour is much more widely used.

So how do I use colour in the garden? As I mentioned in the introduction, I realized how little I knew about the subject when I began using colour. So I went back to looking at how artists use colour and then adapted their ideas in the garden and landscape. I suggest that any designer who really wants to understand this subject should read much more widely than in this short introduction to the subject. There are unfortunately books which promote only one method of using colour, for example monochrome planting, but I would advise readers to look at all possible colour combinations and make up their own minds as to which ones they think most appropriate to the work they are doing.

The colour spectrum

All authorities on colour start with the spectrum, and this is usually drawn as a circle. The colours of the spectrum are the full hues seen in a rainbow, or when light falls through a prism. There are three primary colours – red, blue and yellow – and when two of these are mixed, they create the three secondary colours of purple, orange and green. The spectrum can be seen as just the primary and secondary colours, or expanded by adding any number of intermediate colours between the primary and secondary ones, for example yellow-green, blue-green, orange-red.

To arrive at the thousand or so colours which are distinctly discernible by the human eye, we add white to the full hues to produce tints such as pink, apricot and primrose, and add black to give shades like brown, dark green, navy blue and carmine.

If the spectrum is displayed as a circle with black in the centre and white at the outside, the shades then form circles within the spectral ring and the tints form circles outside. Colour theorists also add that when grey is added to a colour hue, the tones of that colour are produced. This is undoubtedly the case, but within planting design there are few tones which are visually important.

Within the context of the garden, therefore, we do not have a full range of colours at our disposal, there being few shades apart from dark green and the various browns found in trunks and stems of trees and shrubs.

Colour harmonies

Again all, or most, authorities agree on how different colours harmonize, and there are several rules of colour harmony which can work in planting design. These are:

1. The harmony of **adjacent colours**;
2. The harmony of **opposite colours**, also known as **complementary colours**;
3. The harmony of **tints, tones and shades**;
4. The harmony of **triads.**

The harmony of adjacent colours

The rule for this harmony states that colours adjacent to each other in the spectrum form colour harmonies. These harmonies are frequently seen in nature, for example the dark green of wooded hills against a blue sky, the blue of the sky and indigo of the sea and, more spectacularly, the reds and oranges of the sky as the sun sets. We react to these harmonies with an almost visceral pleasure. In all the above instances, the colours are seen as a mass of one colour next to, or

THE SPECTRUM

to show arrangement of Primary, Secondary and Intermediate Colours

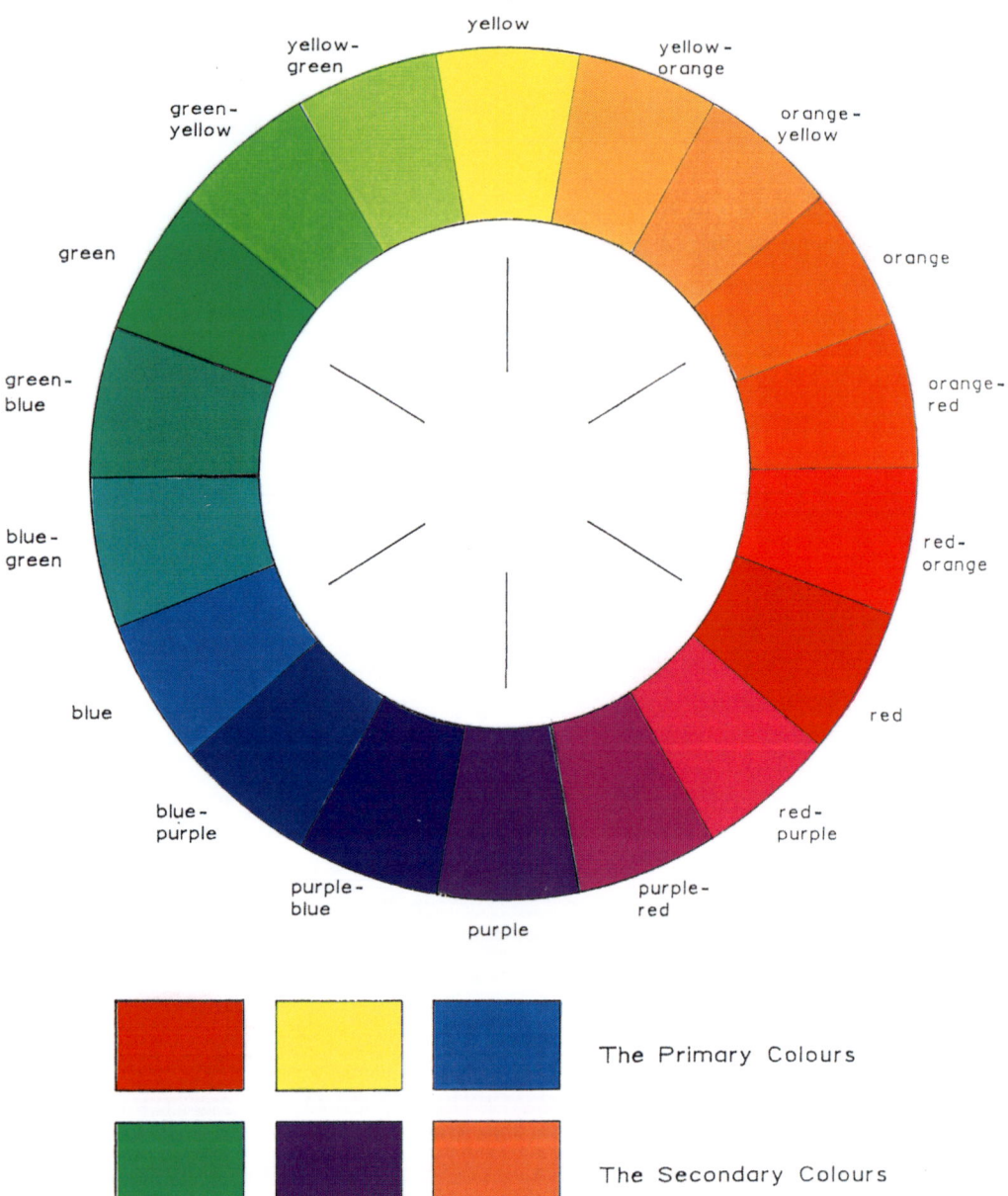

Figure 5.1 The Spectrum — showing primary, secondary and intermediate colours.

intermingling with, a mass of the adjacent colour; this is how these colour harmonies can work best in the landscape and garden. We can consider each harmony in turn:

- *Red with red-purple and red-orange* is seen in the late sunset sky and not easily used in the landscape unless green is eliminated. It can also be seen in the leaf colour of purple and green-leaved shrubs in autumn.

- *Orange with red-orange and yellow-orange* is seen in the early sunset sky and in the autumn colours of trees. I use this harmony in autumn borders where I can combine these flower colours with yellow foliage and autumn colour foliage.

- *Yellow with yellow-orange and yellow-green* are the colours of spring with the yellow-green of new foliage and daffodils. There is green in this harmony, so it can be used for plantings of yellow foliage, green and yellow variegated foliage and yellow flowers. It can give a lovely sunny effect for ground-cover plantings, but is a little boring for ornamental borders without a contrasting colour.

The green colours of the landscape in England.

Sunset colours of red-purple and blue-purple.

Adjacent colour harmonies

- *Green with yellow-green and blue-green* can be seen nowadays most obviously in fields of rape against green hedgerows and distant woods. It is an easy colour harmony for ground-cover planting using green-leaved plants with yellow or blue coloured flowers.

- *Blue with blue-green and blue-purple* are the colour harmonies of water, woodland and sky; bluebell woods are the nearest we get to it in the landscape.

Green with yellow-green planting.

Blue and deep green of bluebell woods.

Red-purple, purple and purple-red colours used in a planting scheme.

Adjacent colours of yellow and yellow-green.

Adjacent colours of red-orange and orange-red.

Adjacent colours of purple and purple-red.

- **Violet with red-purple and blue-purple** takes us back to the late sunset sky just before night falls. I have used this harmony in planting in the Mediterranean where dry conditions mean that there is little grass, or that most plants have grey foliage against which these bright colours look wonderful.

The harmony of opposite, or complementary, colours

This rule states that any two colours directly opposite each other in the spectrum circle will harmonize with each other. These are more exciting harmonies than adjacent ones and work well with small areas of each colour against a neutral background. The easiest opposite colour harmonies to visualize are:

- *Red and green* is seen in many tropical plants. This is an easy harmony to use in the garden, because green leaves can be used with bright red flowers as is the case with some roses.

- *Red-orange and blue-green.* In Australia the blue-green of the predominant eucalyptus is a foil for lots of red-orange or scarlet flowers. If using this harmony in other parts of the globe, look for foliage which is blue-green, and then add the red-orange in flower colour.

- *Orange and blue* is seen most vividly in autumn colour against a bright blue sky. It is not easy to use in the garden until autumn, when bright greens tend to fade and many leaves take on autumn tints.

Red and green — opposite and complementary colours.

Blue and orange — opposite and complementary colours.

Yellow and purple — opposite and complementary colours.

Planting using yellow with blue-purple and purple-red.

- *Yellow-orange and blue-purple.* Think of strelitzias and you have this colour harmony; I suspect it is another one for Australia and with eucalypts.

- *Yellow and purple,* which can be seen in pansies and primroses with violets, is a very attractive harmony. I use it in borders with either the full hues or tints with grey or yellow foliage.

- *Yellow-green and red-purple* is again a tropical colour combination, but more difficult to use in more temperate climates. It is not a combination I have yet tried but it could be very dramatic.

The harmony of tints, tones and shades

This rule states that the tints, tones and shades of a hue harmonize. They are seen very frequently in the landscape where greens range from the bright green of grass to the mid-green of deciduous trees and the dark green of conifers. Planting designers need to appreciate the full range of greens that are at their disposal. But there is a problem when discussing 'green', because there is a paucity of labels to describe it, and there is a range of different greens. Exactly what colour is lime-green, olive-green, or apple-green? The green colours I have seen given those names do not relate to the actual colour of limes, olives or apples and vary widely from one colour source to another. Fortunately it is usually sufficient to group greens into the pure greens, the yellow-greens, the blue-greens and dark greens when using green with other colours. On the other hand, when using the harmony of tints, tones and shades, the designer can play with the full range of greens available.

One can use the tints, tones and shades of other hues but one has to accept that green is usually present. In rose beds where all the foliage is the same dark green, I have used the tints, tones and shades of red, and I have also used the tints, tones and shades of yellow where the foliage is mostly yellow or yellow-green.

The harmony of triads

Here the harmony uses three colours spaced at equal distances around the spectrum. Using the spectrum illustrated there are at least four triad possibilities:

- *The primary colours of red, yellow and blue.* This triad reminds one of the colours of childhood: look at the colours interior designers use when decorating children's rooms. In the landscape it is an unsophisticated harmony and is best seen in spring bedding with red and yellow tulips above a sea of blue forget-me-nots, or of blue gentians with red and yellow primulas against the grass of an alpine meadow. I have not seen it work well in a border, probably because all the flowers need to be full hues of red, yellow and blue and not a variety of tints and full hues.

- *The secondary colours of orange, green and purple.* This is a much more sophisticated triad, and I have used it and seen it used for limited areas of beds particularly at flower shows. I wanted to try it once as the colour scheme for an entire garden at the Chelsea flower show but could not find enough orange spring flowering plants.

- *The intermediate colours of red-orange, yellow-green and blue-purple* provide a fascinating and vibrant combination, and would be worth trying in a mid-summer border. I have frequently used this triad in bedding schemes where it immediately commands attention.

Planting using tints, tones and shades of red-purple with blue-green foliage.

A colourful pot planted in the triad colours of orange, green and purple.

Planting using the opposite and complementary colours of yellow-green and red-purple.

A corner planting of green and white using plants with small flowers.

The striking effect of white tulips standing out against their green background.

- *The intermediate colours of yellow-orange, blue-green and red-purple are probably more suited to the garden than those of the green, orange and purple triad, because they provide a brighter combination. However, they do depend on limiting foliage to blue-green.*

The use of white in planting plans

One of the problems in many otherwise good planting schemes is the inappropriate use of white. White is not a colour as such, and needs to be used with great care. It reflects light, so any large area of white becomes an instant focal point, which is fine if this is the designer's intention, but very distracting if the white is merely part of the overall planting. For this reason it is best to avoid white flowers and white and green variegated foliage in colour borders. If pale colours are needed then use cream, buff or pale blue instead.

For some time there has been a vogue for white gardens. These gardens can be very attractive but need to be planned with care. The best combination is green and white, since it is impossible to have a pure white garden. Use true greens or blue-greens, not yellow-greens, and avoid adding grey foliage as it deadens the impact of the white.

A patch of white plants taking the attention away from the rest of the more muted planting.

Cream-coloured flowers and white and green variegated foliage.

The effect of seasons and sunlight

The other major factor in using colour in planting plans is the effect changing seasons and levels of sunlight have on colour. These factors need to be taken into account when planning seasonal plantings. In temperate climates, the sun is low in intensity in winter, even on a bright day, and the landscape is dominated by the brown of bare branches and the dark green of evergreen plants and conifers. Under these conditions pale colours will glow in the lack of bright light, like the pallid blossoms of the winter flowering cherry, *Prunus subhirtella* 'Autumnalis'. Equally some quite strong colours can work well, such as the vivid pink blossom of the almond, *Prunus dulcis*, which is outstanding as a colour when there are no bright greens to compete with it.

The intensity of the sunlight increases when spring arrives, and the glowing white of the early snowdrops tends to look 'washed out' in these brighter conditions. The yellow-green of new leaves and the bright green of grass need the pale tints of blossom. Primroses and other spring flowers act as a foil, and any spring planting scheme should employ similar colours.

In summer the sun is high in the sky and shines with much greater intensity so that pale colours tend to fade and brighter colours are needed. Full hues look great in strong sunlight, but need to harmonize with the bright greens of summer foliage; good combinations are red flowers as a complementary colour to the greens, or yellow and violet flowers with grey or yellow foliage; also the red-orange, orange and yellow-orange flowers with yellow-green foliage.

The light in autumn is lower in intensity, but it is usually a warm light which shows up the reds, yellows and oranges of autumn foliage. Flowers need to reflect these colours or, using the harmony of opposites, complement them with blue flowers and fruits.

A border in autumn with the bright green foliage of summer changing to the warmer colours of yellow and brown.

Natural colour harmonies

Wherever I have travelled throughout the world looking at native flora, I am constantly struck by the fact that there is always a colour harmony present. The background colours vary as does the intensity of the sun, so that different colour harmonies are possible in different parts of the world.

In tropical areas the vegetation is very lush with large bright green foliage against which there are frequent splashes of red from flowers, stems and leaves and really bright colours are needed to compete. Move to the Mediterranean and there are few greens to be found, because of the heat and dry conditions. Plants need to conserve moisture and, as a result, have small leaves many of which are covered in white hairs and appear grey. In summer it is too dry for grass to grow, and so the background colours are the sandy-coloured soil and the dark grey-green of olive trees, which provide a perfect foil for the strong pinks, blues and purples of cistus, hibiscus and bougainvillea.

In Australia the background colour is the blue-green of the eucalyptus and grey of the soil, and the natural flora includes lots of red, orange and yellow flowers. Contrast this with the high Alps after the snow has melted, which become a patchwork of red, yellow and blue, first against the bare soil and then the bright green of the new grass.

In North America the Rocky Mountains have a background of dark green conifers with the brighter green of aspen leaves in summer, and at this time of year when the snow melts at the edge of the tree line, there are fields of yellow lupins and blue aquilegias. In other parts of the Rockies I have seen fields of red and yellow Indian paintbrushes and yellow rudbeckia colouring the landscape at lower altitudes.

The blue-green colours of Australia with a bright blue sky.

The red and bright green colours of the tropical landscape.

A natural harmony of purple and yellow colours in wild flowers seen in the high Rockies in North America.

In Britain the background colour for most of the year is the bright green of grass with the darker green of deciduous trees. Many native flowers are small woodland ones in pale yellow, pale blue and white, which glow in the shade.

When planning plantings I always look for the natural colour harmonies to help me decide on the most appropriate colour schemes.

Playing with colour harmonies

I am constantly experimenting with colour schemes in my own garden. I have recently tried using black and white. Unfortunately the experiment didn't really work as the result looked forced and rather ugly; so I will not be trying it out on my clients. However, I will keep experimenting. I often start by planting up a container with bedding plants in the colours I want to try together. If I find a scheme where the colours work, I then extend the scheme into larger areas, sometimes using bedding first and then perennials. However, I have found that some colour schemes which work in a container — currently shocking pinks and plum — can be overpowering when enlarged.

Red, orange and brown colours of tulips and wallflowers.

Pink and blue-purple bedding — much loved but can be rather boring.

Red antirrhinums, begonias and pelargoniums with Phormium *'Bronze Baby'.*

Pink tulips and blue forget-me-nots made more exciting with the addition of deep purple-red tulips.

> **Use of colour in planting design**
>
> 1. Keep it simple and if in doubt stick to green.
> 2. Always select a colour scheme for every area.
> 3. Within the wider landscape, don't compete with nature, follow her ideas.
> 4. Experiment with colour and learn from your mistakes.

The cream and plum colours of tulip 'Gavota' matching the emerging foliage of the rose 'Royal William'.

Size

Plants vary from tiny, as in alpine plants like *Soldanella*, to the enormous as in the gigantic redwoods found in northern California. It is important that designers knows the eventual size of all the plants they propose to use. It is easy to underestimate both the size and rate of growth of adjacent plants, so that rather too quickly they can grow into each other and spoil the effect one was trying to create. Books and databases give us the ultimate size of most plants, but the size of an individual plant will vary according to the site conditions, and may vary a great deal from the size possible when the plant grows naturally.

It is also important to know how fast a plant grows. A tree may ultimately reach 30m but may take many years to reach this size, whereas most shrubs may reach their ultimate size in ten years and herbaceous plants in three to five years. In planning plantings, designers need to be able to visualize the size of all the plants chosen in one to three years, at ten years, and then look at the long term to see the results of their planting schemes.

Most plants are available as small specimens, or in small containers, but many clients want an instant effect and are not prepared to wait for plants to grow. Now that

A border planted with pink peonies, purple stachys and red-purple astrantia.

there is a wide range of plants in larger sizes, it is possible to plant for a fairly immediate impact, particularly with herbaceous plants and deciduous shrubs. But it is still not possible, or sensible, to plant many major trees in anything but relatively small sizes. Oak and beech trees, in particular, do not respond well to being planted as large specimens. Designers need to know which sizes are available in the plants included on their planting plans, and whether these will be large enough when planted to satisfy the client expectations.

Using Size

The scale and proportion of a design needs to be balanced by the size of plants and planted areas that are used. Expansive landscapes need large trees, large clumps of shrubs and large planted areas, whereas small cottage gardens will call for small trees and small beds.

Small size

- **Trees** are useful for small gardens, and restricted areas;
- **Conifers** – these are decorative plants for borders or rockeries;
- **Shrubs** – use for low ornamental hedges and in borders;
- **Herbaceous plants** – very small plants like alpines have little impact and need their own beds which may need to be raised;
- **Leaves** give a fine texture;
- **Flowers** have little impact, good for ground cover.

Medium size

- **Trees** are good for general planting and shelter belts;
- **Conifers** are useful for winter colour in shrub groupings;
- **Shrubs** are good for general planting, hedges and borders;
- **Herbaceous plants** are good for borders and ground cover;
- **Leaves** give a medium texture and are useful for general planting;
- **Flowers** are good for borders and colour schemes.

Large size

- **Trees** are used in larger schemes and as focal points;
- **Conifers** are used for tree belts, for focal points and for hedging;
- **Shrubs** are used for tall hedges, shrub groups and backs of borders;
- **Herbaceous plants** are good for impact in borders and naturalistic plantings;
- **Leaves** give a bold texture; use with care;
- **Flowers** give instant impact as border plants or as focal points.

There are some plants which have **extra large sizes**, and these will always form focal points so need to be used with great care; when well placed they can be very dramatic.

A giant plant of Darmera peltata *dwarfing the neighbouring astilbes and hostas.*

A bed planted with several purple foliage plants including Hebe *'Mrs Winder',* Osmanthus heterophyllus *'Purple Shaft' and* Geranium pratense *'Purple Heron' which provide a muted base and background for the bright pink flowers of* Tulipa *'Menton'.*

6 PLANT SELECTION

After the clients have accepted the presentation plan, work will need to start on construction drawings and planting plans so that the garden can be built and planted. On the presentation plan the area to be planted will have been shown but without any detail of what plants will be included in each area. You may already have some ideas for the trees or colour schemes for the ornamental planting, but you still need to select the actual plants. I usually work through the planting in the following order:

1. Trees,
2. Conifers,
3. Shrubs,
4. Hedges,
5. Climbers,
6. Roses,
7. Ground cover,
8. Herbaceous perennials,
9. Bulbs,
10. Annuals and biennials.

Trees

At the outline planning stage I will have indicated trees on my plan, but now they need to have names added; the choice of trees will depend on their function within my design. First and foremost, trees must be selected for their ability to thrive within the soil, aspect and drainage of the site, because they are relatively expensive to buy and plant, and even more expensive to remove and replace if they fail.

Tree belts for shelter and screening are usually native trees where none of the visual qualities are dominant, and the belt itself provides a plain green background with a fine or medium texture.

Structural groups of trees providing lines, avenues and circles are usually chosen for their shape. I usually want vigorous trees with good straight stems, and I need a species which is readily available so that there is a good chance of getting matching specimens.

Focal-point trees may be existing specimens, or if new, then selected for size, shape, habit, leaf colour and occasionally flowers. To be sufficiently striking as a focal point the specimen may need to have at least two strong visual qualities. For a more immediate impact I often suggest that a larger specimen is purchased if the budget allows.

British native deciduous trees

Acer campestre	- Field Maple
Alnus glutinosa	- Alder
Betula pendula	- Silver Birch
Betula pubescens	- Brown Birch
Carpinus betulus	- Hornbeam
Crataegus laevigata	- Midland Hawthorn
Crataegus monogyna	- Hawthorn
Fagus sylvatica	- European Beech
Fraxinus excelsior	- Ash
Malus sylvestris	- Crab Apple
Populus x canescens	- Grey Poplar
Populus nigra	- Black Poplar
Populus tremula	- Aspen
Prunus avium	- Gean or Wild Cherry
Prunus padus	- Bird Cherry
Prunus spinosa	- Sloe
Pyrus communis	- Pear
Quercus petraea	- Sessile Oak
Quercus robur	- Pedunculate Oak
Salix alba	- White Willow
Salix fragilis	- Crack Willow
Sorbus aria	- Whitebeam
Sorbus aucuparia	- Rowan or Mountain Ash
Sorbus torminalis	- Wild Service Tree
Tilia cordata	- Small-leaved Lime
Tilia platyphyllos	- Broad-leaved Lime
Ulmus glabra	- Wych Elm
Ulmus procera	- English Elm

Trees to use as focal points

Trees with a columnar shape:
Fagus sylvatica 'Dawyck'.

Trees with a weeping or pendulous habit:
Alnus incana 'Pendula',
Betula pendula 'Youngii',
Fagus sylvatica 'Pendula',
Fraxinus excelsior 'Pendula',
Salix caprea 'Kilmarnock'.

Trees with coloured leaves:
Acer cappadocicum 'Aureum',
Acer platanoides 'Royal Red',
Catalpa bignonioides 'Aurea',
Fagus sylvatica 'Riversii'.

Fraxinus excelsior 'Pendula'.

A newly-planted avenue of Prunus 'Pink Perfection'.

An arboretum is a collection of interesting specimen trees or groups of trees, and it is arranged so that each tree can be seen. I love planning arboreta as it gives me a chance to plant some of the more interesting and exotic tree species. I may plant trees as single specimens or in small groups of the same species. I allow plenty of room for the individual trees to reach their ultimate size, although within a group I may plant so that the canopies will eventually touch and combine as a single cover. The trees are planted in grass with mown grass paths, allowing all of them to be to be accessed, and I may include glades, avenues and circles of trees for added interest.

Part of an arboretum in Dorset.

Orchards can be planned on the conventional square-grid system with the size of the grid squares dependent on whether standard or half-standard fruit trees are to be planted. I have also planned more informal layouts with the lines of trees staggered or even placed more randomly, but I always space the trees at the same distances apart as in a formal orchard. Check for the pollination requirements of the different varieties and look for an extended fruiting period. I often include damsons, quinces, mulberries and nut trees to add interest to the usual selection of apples, pears, plums and cherries.

Conifers

Native conifers

In Britain we have only three native conifers:

Scots pine *(Pinus sylvestris)*, which is generally associated with upland areas and poorer soils.

Yew *(Taxus baccata)*, which belongs naturally to chalk soils and beech woods.

Juniper *(Juniperus communis)*, is again found on chalk soils and forms a low spreading bush.

All of them are perfectly good plants in their natural habitats, but not particularly good when native plants are needed in our planting schemes. Scots pine, though, can be added to shelter belts and screens, and yew makes an excellent formal hedge.

Dwarf conifers

You either love or hate dwarf conifers in their variety of shapes, habits and textures. In cases where clients want them included, I put a range of them together and add heathers and other fine-textured low plants to form a base. They can also look very attractive planted in conjunction with rocks and informal water features.

Medium-sized conifers

These can be selected for ground cover, screen planting, hedges or for their ornamental value in mixed borders.

Ground cover — there is a range of conifers which have a prostrate or very wide-spreading habit. These provide very useful fine-textured ground cover particularly on slopes and other areas where grass is difficult to cut.

Hedges and screens — some of our best hedging plants are conifers, and many combine evergreen, fine-textured, dense foliage with a fast rate of growth. Leyland cypress (*x Cuprocyparis leylandii*) is the fastest grower, but also needs to be looked after carefully to prevent it getting tall and leggy. It is better as a tall screen but still needs to be regularly trimmed. *Thuja plicata* and *Chamaecyparis lawsoniana* are slightly slower-growing but make much better screens or hedges. All three will act as partial sound barriers against traffic noise. Yew is the best choice for formal hedges, and despite its reputation for being slow-growing, will form a dense hedge quite quickly if bushy plants are planted in good soil at 500mm apart and kept fed and watered.

Ornamental value — there are a great many cultivars of conifers with coloured foliage which can be used to provide all-year-round interest to mixed borders.

Large conifers

I usually include the larger conifers when planning tree-planting schemes and use suitable conifers in tree belts, avenues, circles, as focal points and in arboreta.

Tree belts — the Scots pine is used where native trees are planted, although it is often replaced with Corsican pine (*Pinus nigra*), which looks almost identical when young and is more tolerant of alkaline soils.

The arching needles of **Pinus wallichiana**.

Chaemaecyparis pisifera *'Boulevard'*, an attractive medium-sized conifer which will ultimately reach over 4000mm.

Avenues — I have rarely used conifers for avenues, but I have seen *Cedrus libani* used very effectively, and I have often considered using *Calocedrus decurrens* in a circle. The only problem with the latter is that it takes a considerable time to grow into its typical pencil-like shape.

Focal points — some of the most attractive focal points in large country gardens are mature conifers, particularly the cedars, but they do need plenty of room to be seen at their best, and they need to be in proportion to the size of the house and garden. Those conifers which make good focal points are:

With an oval or columnar shape:

Calocedrus decurrens,
Chamaecyparis lawsoniana 'Columnaris',
Juniperus scopulorum 'Skyrocket',
Taxus baccata 'Fastigiata'.

With an horizontal habit:

Cedrus libani,
Taxus baccata 'Dovastoniana'.

A young Cedrus atlantica, Glauca Group with its characteristic upright habit.

Shrubs

I use shrubs in a variety of ways in my designs:

In front of the trees in a shelter belt — these are always native shrubs often selected for their wildlife potential for food and nesting sites. Some of the most useful are listed in Chapter 3 as shrubs for native hedges.

In informal groups to define spaces — for all-year-round definition, I select evergreen shrubs and use a selection with the same texture and foliage colour.

My favourite **evergreen shrubs for use in structural planting** are:

Aucuba japonica — I only use the plain green varieties
Buxus sempervirens
Camellia japonica — not for shallow chalk soils
Choisya ternata
Cotoneaster frigidus 'Cornubia'
Elaeagnus x ebbingei — a favourite plant for this purpose
Euonymus japonicus — again only the green form
Ilex x altaclarensis
Ilex aquifolium
Ligustrum lucidum — this is the best ligustrum
Mahonia japonica
Osmanthus heterophyllus
Photinia x fraseri 'Red Robin'
Prunus laurocerasus
Prunus lusitanica
Viburnum tinus

To give height to beds and borders, and to extend the season of interest — these shrubs are selected for flower and foliage colour and possibly for texture.

In rows as avenues to define vistas — I use shrubs for defining vistas where space is limited or the scale too small for trees. Shrubs are selected for good shape, habit, colour or texture or a combination of these.

As focal points — for small areas, the shrub needs to have a strong shape, habit or colour or combination of two of these.

Viburnum sargentii 'Onondaga', a shrub which has purple-red young foliage with red buds opening to white flowers, followed by red berries and red-purple autumn foliage. It is a useful plant for mixed borders providing colour from spring till late autumn.

Shrubs which make good focal points:

With a spiky shape and coloured foliage:

Cordyline australis 'Torbay Red' — not fully hardy;
Phormium cookianum 'Sundowner';
Yucca filamentosa 'Bright Edge'.

With a weeping habit:

Cotoneaster 'Hybridus 'Pendulus'.

With an horizontal habit:

Cornus controversa 'Variegata';
Viburnum plicatum 'Mariesii'.

Hedges

A hedge is a row of trees or shrubs planted closely together in a line to form a uniform texture and then trimmed as necessary. The plants selected need to thrive in the site conditions, and grow well when planted closely together or enjoy being regularly pruned. The choice of hedging plants will depend on the function of the hedge.

Native hedges — these have been covered in detail in Chapter 3.

Boundary hedges — these may consist of native shrubs and trees, but more often they divide neighbouring properties. What is needed is a dense boundary which may need to keep dogs and children in or out, or may be needed to act as a sound barrier, or to hide the neighbour's washing. The plant chosen needs to be tough, non-poisonous and usually evergreen, but the final selection depends on the height required, space available and ultimately the client's wishes.

Internal division — the choice of plant will depend on the style of the garden and, again, the client's preference. Invariably I like to use yew for formal gardens, and beech or hornbeam in less formal situations.

Informal flowering hedges — I use these to form divisions in less formal parts of the garden and to screen functional areas like vegetable gardens and tennis courts. The shrubs are planted in a row but only trimmed if they get too untidy, so that the overall effect is more rounded than trimmed hedges. There is a range of good flowering plants which grow well when planted close together, and often provide colourful fruit as well as flowers. I used to mix species within the hedge, but now prefer the look of a single species.

Ornamental hedges as edging or as parterres and knot gardens — the plants chosen need to be evergreen, fine-textured and capable of surviving close clipping at a low height. I tend to use box (*Buxus sempervirens*) for most low hedging; traditionally this was always used for parterres. Knot gardens consist of a mixture of low hedges and cotton lavender (*Santolina chamaecyparissus*), wall germander (*Teucrium chamedrys*), box and lavender (*Lavandula angustifolia*). I now include some of the smaller hebes instead of lavender, as they are easier to keep in good shape.

A lavender hedge in front of a rose bed.

Pyracatha trained along wires to break up an expanse of brick wall.

The self-clinging climber Parthenocissus quinquefolia *climbing around windows.*

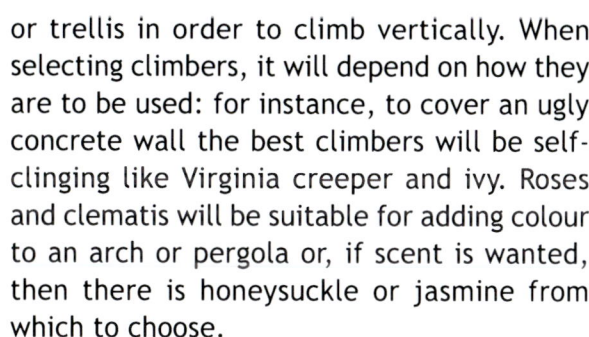

Climbers

Most of my clients will want some climbing plants, for screening, for covering walls and pergolas, or because of their scent or flowers. True climbers, as opposed to wall shrubs — which are shrubs that can be trained against a wall — need support to climb, and without it will grow horizontally along the ground. As such, several of them can be used as ground cover, for example ivy. Climbers can be divided into those which are self-clinging and have suckers and, if planted against a wall or fence, will climb up unaided; and those which have tendrils or twining stems and, given a trellis or wires on a wall, will climb without much assistance. Then there are climbers, such as the climbing roses, which rely on their downward pointing thorns to hold on to adjacent plants. These need tying on to wires or trellis in order to climb vertically. When selecting climbers, it will depend on how they are to be used: for instance, to cover an ugly concrete wall the best climbers will be self-clinging like Virginia creeper and ivy. Roses and clematis will be suitable for adding colour to an arch or pergola or, if scent is wanted, then there is honeysuckle or jasmine from which to choose.

The climbers I plant most frequently include:

Species	Habit	Orientation
Clematis montana	tendrils	any aspect
Hedera colchica (evergreen)	self-clinging	any aspect
Hydrangea anomala subsp. petiolaris	self-clinging	any aspect
Jasminum officinale	partial twining	sun to light shade
Lonicera japonica (semi-evergreen)	twining stems	any aspect
Parthenocissus quinquefolia	self-clinging	any aspect
Trachelospermum jasminoides (evergreen)	needs tying in	sun to light shade
Wisteria floribunda	twining stems	sun

When a client wants a range of climbers, but there are no suitable walls, I may suggest building a pergola or series of arches to allow for planting their favourite varieties.

Clematis montana, *the most reliable clematis and the easiest to grow.*

A well-trained wisteria *beginning to cover a large wall.*

Roses

Roses are shrubs, but they are so numerous and diverse that they are usually considered as a separate group of plants. Most rose species and cultivars cross readily with each other, and this has given rise to literally hundreds of different roses with rose nurseries introducing new cultivars each year. All roses, except the species roses, are propagated vegetatively, and any inherent weakness is carried through to new plants and eventually may lead to a decrease in the vigour of the rose. I have known this happen in only three years with a cultivar produced especially for one of the gardens I designed for a Chelsea Flower Show, so I do not include any new rose, however beautiful, until it has been around for several years and proved its vigour. Roses can be divided into the following groups:

- Species roses,
- Shrub roses,
- Bedding roses,
- English roses,
- Climbing roses,
- Rambler roses.

Species roses

There are 150 different rose species growing wild around the world, including three native to Britain: the dog rose *Rosa canina*, the field rose *Rosa arvensis*, both of which are frequently found in hedgerows, and the burnet rose *Rosa spinosissima*, frequently found in sand dunes or along the seashore. Species roses flower only once, but may then produce attractive hips in the autumn. Species roses can be used for informal hedges, e.g. *Rosa rugosa*; for shrub groupings in large mixed borders, e.g. *Rosa glauca*; as ground cover, e.g. *Rosa paulii*; and many have an attractive habit which makes them useful as specimen shrubs in long grass areas, e.g. *Rosa moyesii*.

Shrub roses

Shrub roses have been bred from crossing rose species and rose hybrids, or more recently bedding roses. They include roses that flower once a year and those which flower almost continuously from midsummer through to late autumn. As a rule shrub roses do not need pruning and are resistant to pests and diseases. They can be used like rose species for informal hedges, in shrub groupings, in mixed borders and as specimen shrubs. The taller ones can be trained against fences, and there are many which have been bred specifically as ground-cover roses.

Bedding roses are usually seen in rose beds and have been bred for maximum flower impact. They share the following characteristics:

- The flowers appear almost continuously from midsummer to late autumn;
- They need pruning each year to maintain vigour;
- They need to be sprayed regularly to control pests and disease;
- They need regular feeding to maintain growth.

They include:

Hybrid tea roses, which have large flowers, usually of a conical shape in bud and frequently with a single flower per stem. They are generally taller than floribundas and some are richly fragrant. They are useful for the middle rows in rose beds.

Floribunda roses have clusters of flowers, are lower growing and, frequently, are lacking in fragrance; useful for the outside rows of rose beds.

Patio roses were first introduced in the 1960s and are smaller, more compact plants, but otherwise similar to floribunda roses and useful where a smaller rose is needed.

Planting bedding roses

Bedding roses are best planted in beds without other plants, except for an edging row of low herbaceous plants, for example *Geranium himalayense*. Beds can be informal but are usually formal in shape. Roses prefer a rich, clay loam but will grow in most soils if plenty of organic matter is added. They grow best in the eastern parts of Britain, but are suitable for all areas except the far west.

The hybrid tea rose 'Just Joey'.

Planning rose beds

- Allow 600mm spacing between roses (450mm for patio roses);
- Allow for a row of edging plants at 450mm apart;
- Use standard roses for extra height or interest;
- Restrict colours preferably to one colour per bed.

English roses are recent introductions bred by David Austin, and are the result of crossing shrub roses with bedding roses. Bred for beauty, health and vigour, they require less pruning, feeding and spraying than the bedding roses, and can be planted in rose beds or in mixed borders. They have now been around long enough to have proved their viability, and I am now using them in rose beds rather than bedding roses.

Climbing roses are climbing sports of some of the shrub, bedding and English roses, and have larger, usually double, flowers in a range of colours. The stems are stiff, and growth is relatively low compared with ramblers. They require pruning and training on to wires annually, and may need spraying to control pests and diseases. They are very useful for walls, trellis, pillars and the stronger ones for pergolas.

'Albertine', among the loveliest and most reliable of rambling roses and can grow up to 6000mm high.

'Gloire de Dijon', a buff-coloured climbing rose which flowers nearly continuously during the summer and grows to 4000mm high.

The English rose 'William Shakespeare'.

Ramblers include species roses and roses bred from climbers which naturally produce long shoots and climb other plants by hanging on to their branches using their downward pointing thorns. They are once-flowering with clusters of mostly white or pink flowers and often produce hips. They can be very vigorous, growing up to 15m, and are only pruned to control spread. They are useful for growing up through trees, for large pergolas or high walls.

Ground cover

As already stated, ground cover shown on the presentation plan may include grass areas as:

Mown grass, which may be sown using a suitable seed mixture, or laid as turf chosen appropriately for the site. The selection of grasses will depend on the desired quality of the lawn and how much wear it is going to get. The decision is always whether to include perennial rye grass in the seed mixture; it is fast-growing and resistant to wear and tear, but not suitable for a formal lawn which is to be cut with a cylinder mower. I always include it in the mix where the owners have children who will use the mown grass areas for football practice or other games.

Longer grass — again, use a suitable seed mixture depending on the intended mowing regime.

Wildflower meadows — use a suitable seed mixture or add plugs to the existing sward. There are several specialist nurseries where advice can be had on which plants would be suitable for a specific location.

Lamium maculatum which is not quite as vigorous as Lamium galeobdolon *but a good alternative if using a silver/pink/blue colour scheme.*

Other plants are used as ground cover and can be planted in a range of different areas which include:

Carpet bedding — these need to be selected from a range of low-growing plants suitable for this purpose;

Parterres and knot gardens — see details under hedges above;

Drifts of a single species — already mentioned under conifers, but there are many suitable plants which need to be selected for the soil, amount of sunlight and drainage to be sure that they will grow vigorously and completely cover the designated area.

Over the years I have used a range of different plants as ***drifts of a single species*** and they include:

Calluna vulgaris	- needs acid soil
Cornus canadensis	- needs acid soil
Cotonester dammeri	
Erica carnea	
Galium odoratum	
Gaultheria shallon	- needs acid soil
Geranium macrorrhizum	
Hedera helix	
Hypericum calycinum	- now a problem with rust
Juniperus horizontalis	
Lamium galeobdolon	
Lonicera nitida	
Rubus tricolor	
Symphytum officinale	
Vinca minor	

Woodland and woodland-edge planting — select native plants found in woodlands in line with the soil and drainage of your site. Frequently woodland plants are found in large drifts of low-growing plants, such as wood anemone (*Anemone nemorosa*) with occasional groups of taller plants like foxgloves (*Digitalis purpurea*). Alternatively plant drifts of other suitable plants or even work with a matrix.

Waterside and wetlands — I place drifts of plants selected on whether the soil is constantly moist, wet or covered in water. The most problematic areas are those which are wet in winter and dry out in summer, but there are one or two native plants which seem to cope with these conditions, and they are:

Filipendula ulmaria	- meadowsweet
Iris pseudacorus	- yellow flag
Lythrum salicaria	- purple loosestrife

Frequently where the clients are not keen gardeners, but want some colour and seasonal interest in their garden, I use ground-cover plants in beds and borders, as it entails less weeding. Used in this way it becomes part of the ornamental planting.

Meadowsweet (Filipendula ulmaria) *with purple loosestrife* (Lythrum salicaria) *in the background.*

Herbaceous perennials

These are non-woody plants that generally, but not always, produce leaves and flowers each year and die down in the winter. They provide us with native plants for woodland, woodland edge and wetland, as ground-cover plantings which can be formal or informal; also as plants used in herbaceous and mixed borders. They range in size from 20mm to 2000mm high and come in all colours, shapes and sizes, and include some of the best-known border plants like delphiniums, lupins, and oriental poppies which have provided the main source of summer colour for traditional herbaceous borders. The problem with these particular plants is that they are quite difficult to grow, they frequently need staking and they may need dividing every three to five years. When my clients or their gardeners have the necessary expertise and want to look after these plants, I still include them in my planting schemes, but more frequently I look for border plants which require less work and are more likely to survive.

In any planting scheme I will be looking for **front-of-border plants** which I will select for their foliage as much as for their flowers. My favourites include:

Alchemilla mollis,
Anthemis tinctoria 'E.C.Buxton',
Astrantia major 'Hadspen Blood',
Bergenia 'Silberlicht',
Coreopsis grandiflora,
Geranium himalayense 'Gravetye',
Geranium renardii,
Geranium sanguineum,
Geum 'Borisii',
Heuchera 'Plum Puddin',
Nepeta x faassenii,
Origanum onites 'Aureum',
Osteospermum jucundum 'Compactum',
Polemonium caeruleum,
Salvia nemorosa 'Ostfriesland',
Sedum spectabile 'Brilliant',
Sisyrinchium striatum.

Geranium renardii, a reliable plant for the front of a bed or border.

I then will need plants *for the middle of the beds and borders,* and here the flower is more important than foliage. I usually include some of the following plants:

Agapanthus campanulatus,
Aquilegia 'Blue Barlow',
Aster x frikartii 'Mönch',
Campanula persicifolia,
Crocosmia 'Lucifer',
Echinacea purpurea,
Hemerocallis 'Gentle Shepherd',
Iris germanica,
Leucanthemum maximum 'Esther Read',
Paeonia lactiflora,
Penstemon 'Andenken an Friedrich Hahn',
Phlox paniculata,
Rudbeckia fulgida 'Goldsturm',
Scabiosa caucasica,
Tradescantia x andersoniana.

Papaver orientale *'Perry's White', which is a wonderful sight in full bloom, but its foliage dies soon after and needs an adjacent plant which will cover it up in late summer.*

I may also need some taller herbaceous perennials *for the back of the border*, which I select for height and habit as well as flower colour:

Achillea filipendula 'Gold Plate',
Aconitum carmichaelii 'Arendsii',
Anemone x hybrida 'Honorine Jobert',
Campanula lactiflora 'Loddon Anna',
Epilobium angustifolium 'Album',
Helenium 'Moerheim Beauty',
Knautia macedonica,
Thalictrum aquilegiifolium,
Verbena bonariensis,
Veronicastrum 'Temptation'.

Penstemon *'Andenken an Friedrich Hahn', which used to have the much easier name to pronounce, 'Garnet', and is the most reliable of the penstemons for the border.*

Phlox paniculata *'Norah Leigh', which has bright pink flowers and attractive variegated foliage as an added extra.*

Grasses — When I first started planting gardens, there were very few grasses readily available, and these were Pampas grass (*Cortaderia selloana*), which is not easy to place attractively; *Festuca glauca*, which is too blue and rigid unless you can get just the right plants to plant with it; and 'Gardeners Garters' (*Phalaris arundinacea*), which tends to take over any area in which it is planted. It is only in more recent years that grasses have come into their own, and there are now plenty that make attractive border plants. I find grasses planted on their own are rather boring — too much harmony of texture — but I now include them in many of my planting schemes and have found that they make good plant associations with taller herbaceous plants with daisy-shaped flowers. I think this is because the ray petals of the daisy echo the linear texture of the grasses. I also plant grasses and some of the tall herbaceous plants that produce open inflorescences of small flowers like *Verbena bonariensis*, *Knautia macedonica* and *Cephalaria gigantea*, choosing grasses of the same height as the herbaceous plants. Alternatively I plant smaller grasses with other plants with a linear texture like *Sisyrinchium striatum*, *Iris pallida* 'Variegata', *Asphodeline lutea*, or *Kniphofia* 'Little Maid' and find this works well.

Grasses I use frequently include:

Calamagrostis x acutiflora 'Overdam',
Deschampsia cespitosa 'Bronzeschleijer',
Deschampsia flexuosa 'Tatra Gold',
Miscanthus sinensis 'Morning Light',
Molinia caerulea,
Phalaris arundinacea 'Feesey' — this seems to be a less invasive form,
Stpa calamagrostis,
Stipa gigantea.

Sedges *Carex* spp. and woodrushes *Luzula* spp. are botanically distinct from grasses but visually they look very similar, and I mix them in with grasses when appropriate. My favourite **sedges** include:

Carex elata 'Aurea',
Carex oshimensis 'Evergold',
Carex 'Silver Sceptre',
Luzula sylvatica 'Marginata'.

Where the border is in **shade**, my plant list may well include some of the following herbaceous plants:

Bergenia 'Silberlicht',
Brunnera macrophylla 'Jack Frost',
Dicentra formosa,
Epimedium perralchicum 'Frohnleiten',
Euphorbia amygdaloides var.*robbiae*,
Geranium nodosum,
Geranium phaeum 'Samobor',
Helleborus x hybridus
Hosta 'Honeybells' — hostas are always a little risky to plant because of snails,
Iris foetidissima,
Lamium orvala,
Liriope muscari,
Pulmonaria saccharata.

Stipa gigantea, *which is a more elegant specimen grass than* Cortaderia selloana.

I will usually add **ferns** to my plant selection for shade borders and some of the best are:

Asplenium scolopendrium,
Cyrtomium falcatum,
Dryopteris affinis,
Dryopteris filix-mas,
Polystichum aculeatum,
Polystichum setiferum.

The hart's tongue fern, Asplenium scolopendrium, *one of our native ferns among the easiest to grow.*

Bulbs

These are the plants usually planted in autumn to flower the following spring, and include daffodils, tulips, hyacinths, crocus and scillas. Some bulbs, particularly narcissus, scillas and crocus, will come up year after year, and are frequently planted in areas of long grass and left to naturalize. The bulbs are usually planted in the autumn following the establishment of the grass. Bulbs can also be planted in containers on their own, with spring bedding plants like pansies, or they can be planted in groups in beds and borders. In containers or borders many of the bulbs, particularly tulips and hyacinths, will need replacing regularly as they tend to become less vigorous each succeeding year. If bulbs are to be planted in the borders, I give the client instructions on when to replant and with which varieties.

Black and white tulips add drama to a bed of green and dark plum foliage.

Annuals and biennials

Annuals grow from seed and flower, fruit and die within the first year, whereas biennials grow from seed in the first year and form a clump of leaves; they flower in the second year and then die. Annuals need to be planted each year and biennials every second year, so I do not include them in any planting scheme unless the client, or their gardener, is prepared to do this. As consultant to a few public gardens, where the policy is to have displays of annuals in the summer and bulbs and biennials for the spring, I prepare lists of suitable plants each year and regularly change the colour scheme. I try out new colour schemes in containers in my own garden first and then as bedding schemes for these clients. Lastly, if really successful, I use the colour scheme with perennial plants.

The hardy annual, Nigella damascena, *which can be left to seed itself in a border.*

Lists of possible plants

Next I prepare a list of potential plants to include within my plan. You may be able to do this from your acquired knowledge, but most of us resort to databases, our library, favourite catalogues, existing lists and previous plans. Start selecting suitable plants, and add their colour and height to the name unless you know them really well. This is particularly important when using unfamiliar species and cultivars. Always check hardiness and the soil, light and moisture requirements of plants you do not know. Some books mix a whole range of plants of different hardiness under the guise of the same flower colour, so check, check and double check. We have had 14 relatively mild winters at the start of the millennium due perhaps to global warming, or just because there has not been a really cold period. The result is that many varieties that were too tender to plant in British gardens years ago have been regularly planted nowadays and are readily available. However, the winters of 2011 and 2012 were much colder, and many of these plants were killed. So it is back to the safety of using plants which are fully hardy, and placing more tender plants — as I was originally taught — against a south-facing wall in the warmer parts of the country. A designer is being negligent when selecting plants that are unlikely to thrive in the given conditions. In your own garden you are at liberty to risk using plants in sites in which they may not survive, but never in a client's garden.

It is also useful to remember that rare and unusual plants have those qualities precisely because they are difficult to grow, so experiment with these in your own garden and not in your client's. Rare plants may be difficult to find and, unless your clients have requested a particular plant, it is unfair to them, their gardener or their contractor to select plants which can only be found in a few nurseries. It is much safer to stick to plants you know you can find or those which, in the *RHS Plant Finder*, are designated as widely available.

If my clients are keen gardeners, and either know their plants or are prepared to look them up, I often send them my list of potential plants so that I can be reasonably sure that they are happy with my choice before I prepare the planting plan. This avoids making too many changes in the plan, which can be very time-consuming.

Plant associations

The key to good planting design is to create a series of attractive plant associations, which are plant groupings that visually belong together, and this is achieved by selecting adjacent plants which have a least one visual quality in common and one different. If all the visual qualities are the same, the plants look very similar and you might as well use all plants of the same variety. If all visual qualities are different, the plants literally quarrel with each other, and the planting looks a mess.

Euphorbia characias *'Tasmanian Tiger'* and Sedum telephium *'Purple Emperor'*, *whose leaves have a similar texture, but the startlingly different coloured leaves make a dramatic contrast.*

Alchemilla mollis *and* Euphorbia characias *with similarly coloured foliage and flowers but differently shaped foliage and size.*

I always start by deciding on a colour scheme, and then decide whether I want to include plants with a similar texture, flower shape or habit. This will help to create a basic harmony to the planting. When using a colour scheme of two flower colours, then two adjacent plants will probably be chosen for these two colours, for example a yellow flower next to a purple one, and they will need to have a common visual quality to form a good association. For front-of-border plants this quality might be similar foliage texture and colour, and in plants for the middle of the border it might be flower shape. With back-of-border plants it might be flower habit and/or shape. In beds or drifts of ground cover with plants of the same height, and where the flowers are of secondary importance, I might select a similar texture for all the plants and then contrast the foliage colour. Although the flowers may not be important, it is necessary to check that they fit in with your colour scheme.

I often find it easier to create attractive plant associations when the site or the client requirements restrict the range of plants I can use. Very shady sites can be lovely since many shade plants have large leaves to absorb as much light as possible, and they tend to look good together. Very hot dry sites need plants with small leaves, or leaves covered in hairs which reduce transpiration, and again look great together.

The long yellow ray florets of Rudbeckia *'Goldsturm' echo the linear leaves of the irises behind.*

The unfurling habit of Matteucia struthiopteris *mimicked by the curling edge of the the flowers of* Erythronium dens-canis *'Pagoda'.*

PLANT ASSOCIATIONS 81

An attractive planting of blue aquilegia and white myosotis, with the starry flowers of Astrantia major *and* Allium christophii.

Hosta *'Honeybells'*, Hosta undulata *var.* albomarginata, Acanthus spinosus *and* Aegopodium podagraria *'Variegatum' create an harmonious planting of white and green.*

7 PLANTING PLANS

The objective of the presentation plan for a garden or landscaped area is to show the lines and design of the proposal as attractively as possible and, to this end, colour is often added to the plan and interesting symbols are used all in an effort to have our proposals accepted by the client. The greater the clarity of the plan so the easier it is for the client to understand and appreciate the ideas shown on it.

Once the overall plan has been accepted, it then needs to be implemented and probably a range of working drawings produced. These frequently include planting plans to show which plants are to be used and exactly where they are to be placed.

I tend to include the tree names on the overall plan, unless there is to be a woodland area or an arboretum which need more detail than can easily be included on this plan. For all other planting I produce detailed planting plans, and these must be accurate, clear and unambiguous. The planting plan or plans will be part of the contract documents for the contractor, and any mistake can be costly in time and money for, if due to designer error, the designer may have to pick up the bill.

Scales to use for planting plans

The plans are the working documents which enable the contractor — or the client — to accurately and easily place the plants chosen by the designer. To allow this to be done without too many problems, the plan needs to be drawn to a large enough scale so that there is room to show each plant to be placed. It hardly needs saying that this needs to be a recognizable scale that is found on most scale rules.

Most of my planting plans are drawn at a scale of 1:50, the exceptions being for arboreta and woodland where I may use a scale of 1:100. However, this only allows for relatively simple underplanting of the trees such as large drifts of one species. I use a scale of 1:20 or 1:25 for show gardens, as the planting is much denser than for other gardens and needs a larger scale for greater clarity; I may also use this scale for small herb gardens and alpine beds.

Drawing planting plans

The planting plan needs to include sufficient detail of the rest of the garden to allow the bed, or planted area, to be set out in the correct position. So I always put in the outline of paths, walls, fences and other features, but without any unnecessary detail, such as paving or brickwork, as these can look fussy and detract from the planting detail. I add any existing planting, including trees which I draw showing the diameter of the trunk at ground level and the full spread of the canopy, as both of these will affect where plants can be placed. I then add any services above or below ground as these will also affect where plants can be positioned. All areas to be planted need to be drawn to show all their edges, proposed or existing.

The planting plan also needs to include, as with all other plans, a north sign and a box at the bottom or in the corner with the following details:

1. The designer's name, address, telephone number and email address;
2. The client's name and/or house name — but not their full address;
3. Name of the job, which will also appear on all plans for the same client;
4. The name of the drawing, e.g. 'Planting Plan for Herb Garden';
5. The scale used plus a bar scale;
6. The date — I use only the month and year;
7. A drawing number which includes the job number plus the number for the planting plan and room for revisions to be added.

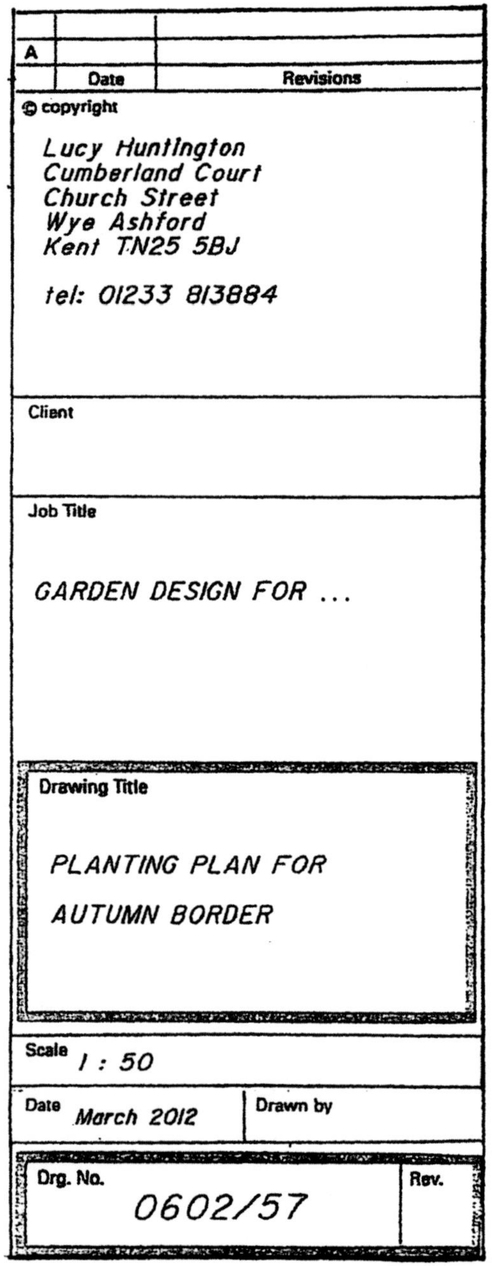

Figure 7.1 *The box in the corner of the planting plan. Here the client's name has been removed to maintain confidentiality.*

The use of circles on the planting plan

Clarity is essential and there is no place on a planting plan for pretty symbols or colour, instead plain circles, drawn with a circle template, are used for each plant with a central cross to indicate exactly where each plant is to be planted.

Groups of the same species are shown as linked circles – see Fig 7.2. I originally added lines to link these circles but I found that the lines could cause confusion and now never add them. The circles should touch and not overlap, as the overlapping lines can confuse but also indicate that the plants should be planted closer together than intended. The diameter of the circle is dictated by the ultimate spread of the plant and, to a lesser extent, its position in the bed.

Naming plants on the planting plan

Within each circle, or group of circles, the number of plants is indicated and the full botanical name of the plant written. Excessively long plant names, such as *Acer palmatum* var. *dissectum* 'Red Autumn Lace', may prove quite difficult or almost impossible to label in full. Nevertheless it is the only acceptable way of showing which plants are to be planted where with any degree of clarity. Many of my students over the years have complained at having to write the plant names on their plans, yet I have never had a single complaint from contractors or gardeners when I have done it! Sometimes, with exceptionally long names I may use an abbreviation but, as I always accompany a planting plan with a plant list, I will then indicate on this list where I have used an abbreviation: for example, *Acer palmatum* var. *dissectum* 'Red Autumn Lace' can be labelled *Acer palmatum dis.* 'Red Autumn Lace'. I never, ever use arrows on planting plans: they may look very attractive to the graphic designer, but they only lead to confusion when planting a border on a wet, windy day in winter.

Figure 7.2 *Circles on planting plans.*

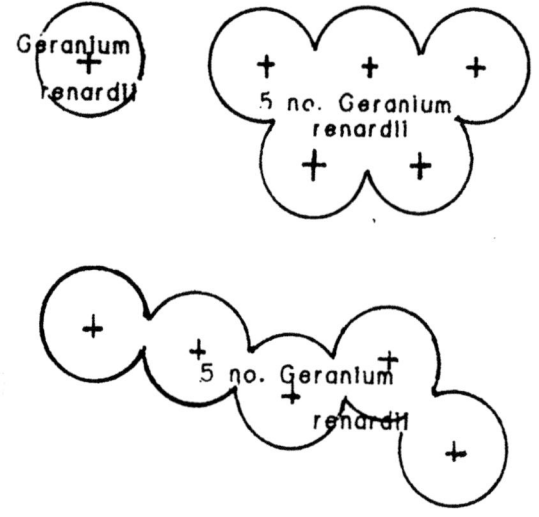

Some colleges still promote this form of labelling on planting plans, and I can only assume that the lecturers have never actually had contractors carry out one of their planting plans. If they had they would realize just how impossible it is to follow. Even lazier, are planting designers who use a key so that the contractor has constantly to be checking where each plant is on the plan, and in desperation writing down the plant names on the plan before starting to plant. Much time, aggravation and confusion can be saved by the designer writing the names on the plan in the first place!

The worst offenders in the bad planting plan stakes are designers who fill up the proposed border with irregular shapes, and then place a number of plants in each blob, leaving the contractor or gardener to work out where individual plants are to be placed. It would serve a designer right if a contractor were to place all the plants in one corner of the blob on the basis that he or she had not been told differently. By all means start the planting plan with oval shapes or long drifts as you work through your planting ideas, and temporarily colour these if you wish, but then you should translate it all into a professional planting plan with names and numbers of the plants within circles.

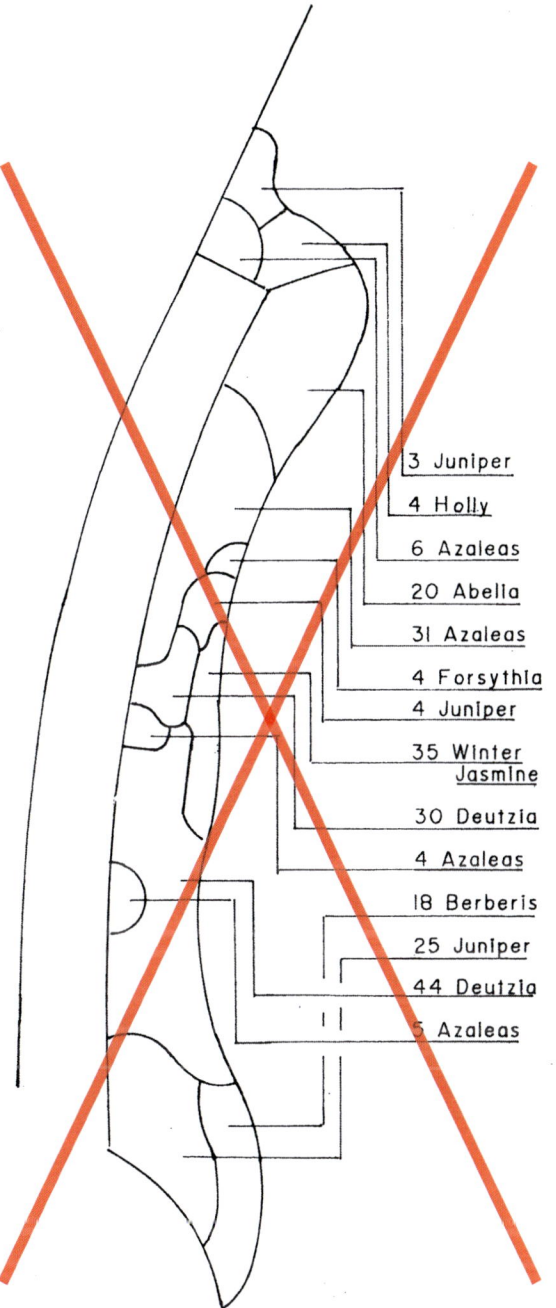

Figure 7.3 An unintelligible plan.
The plan is hard to follow and gives no indication of plant spacings or actual species to be planted.

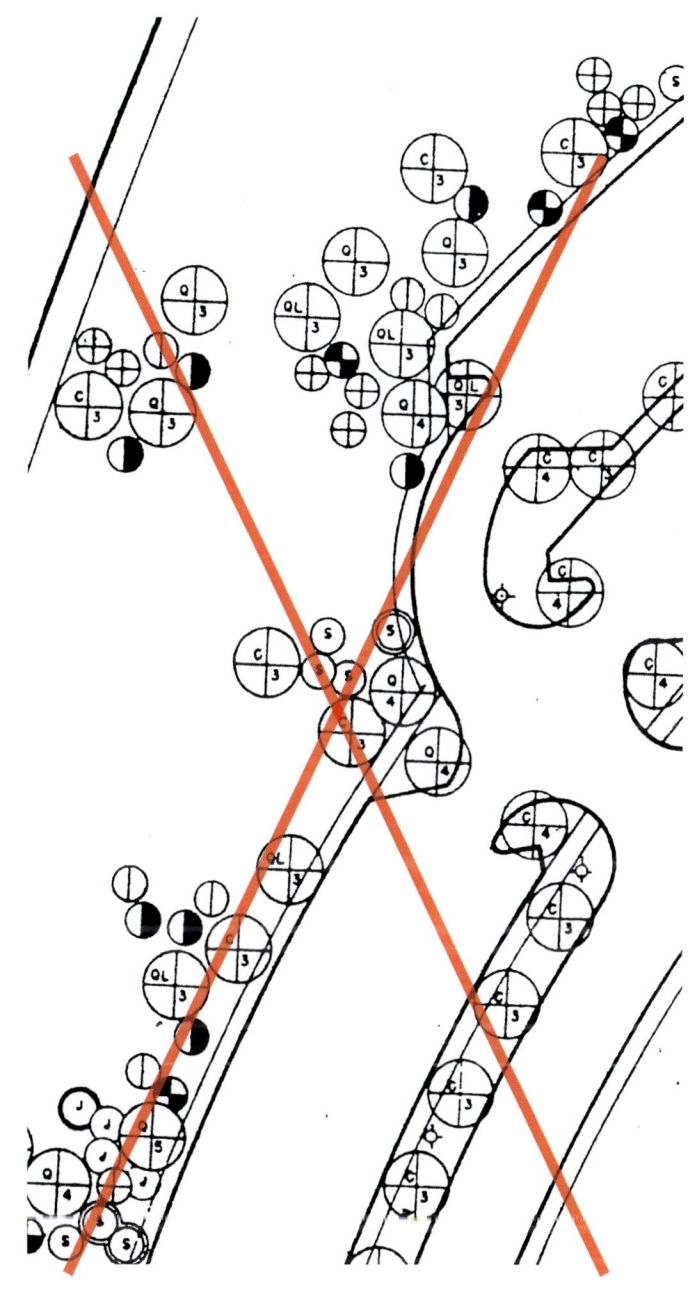

Figure 7.4 Another unintelligible plan.
The designer has used a range of symbols for trees, but it requires a key to decode the plan, which was not attached to it.

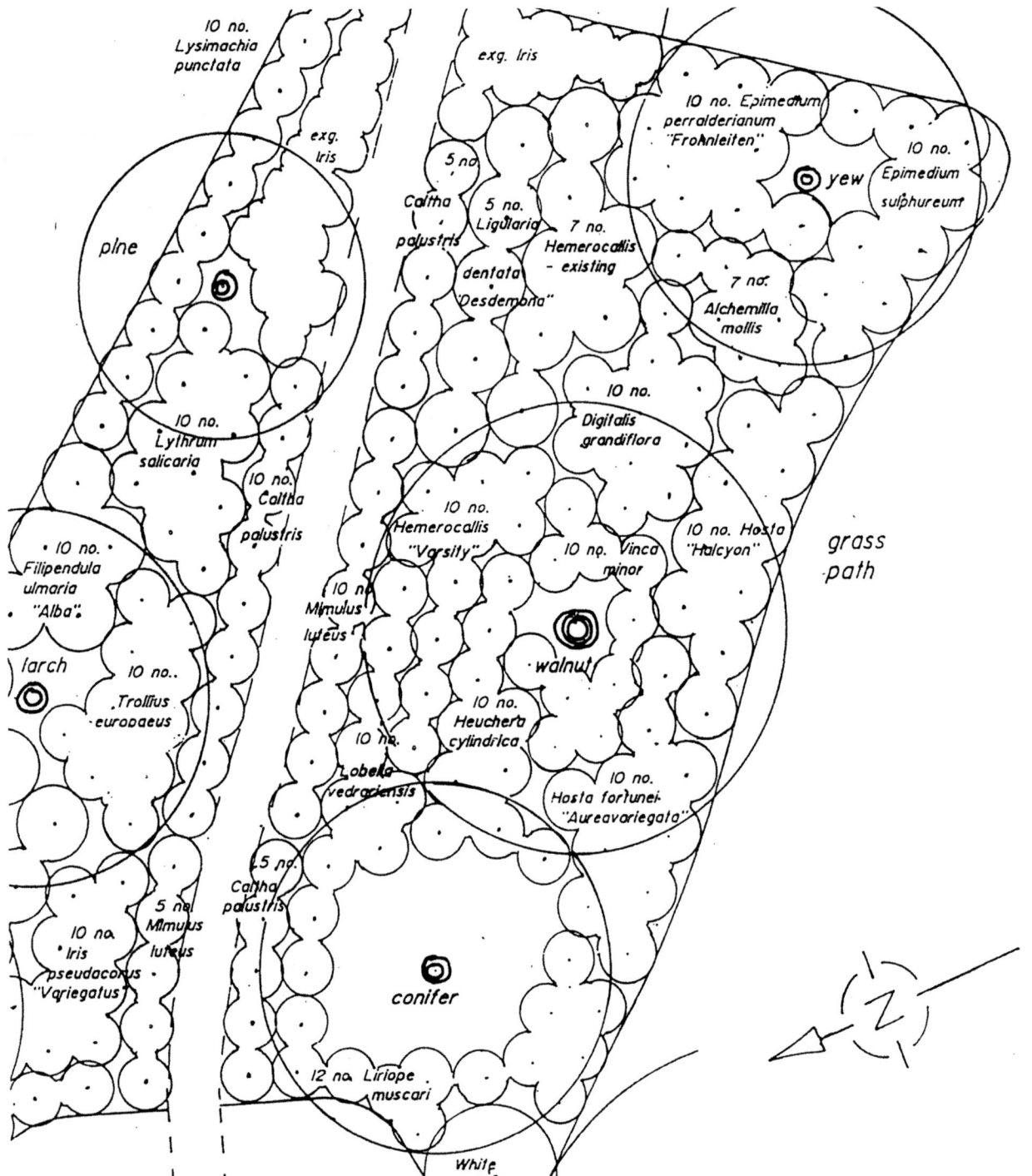

Figure 7.5 Part of a planting plan for streamside beds. The plan is drawn using a scale of 1 : 50, and it is very clear how many of each plant are to be used and exactly where they are to be placed.

Plant spacings

When I started producing planting plans I would look up each plant and note its ultimate size, or size after five years, and then draw a circle of that size. However, this meant that I needed to check each plant, and it became difficult to plan a border in one piece, as I had to keep changing the size of area for each group of plants. I then started teaching planting design and realized that plant spacing was an area which needed simplifying. The various reference books, if they gave any indication of plant spacing at all, gave a variety of different planting distances, sometimes directly converted from Imperial measurements so that 15in became 38cm, which is impossible to work with. How many of us readily know our 38-times table? Other books and catalogues gave just the ultimate spread without necessarily indicating how long it might take the plant to reach it. Yet other books indicated the number of plants needed per square metre, but to allow flexibility such as 5 to 7 per square metre. So I decided to set out some standard spacings which would apply to a whole range of plants.

Plant spacings

Type of plant	Plant spacing	Plants per m
Tree - large	8000mm	-
Tree - medium	5000mm	-
Tree - smal	3000mm	-
Shrub - vigorous	1500mm	-
Shrub - medium	1000mm	1
Shrub - small	600mm	3
Roses - shrub	1200mm	1
Roses - bedding	600mm	3
Herbaceous - large	600mm	3
Herbaceous - medium	450mm	5
Herbaceous - small	300mm	10
Ground cover - vigorous	600mm	3
Ground-cover plants - medium	450mm	5
Heathers	450mm	5
Climbers - vigorous	3000mm	-
Climbers - medium	2000mm	-
Annuals	200mm	25
Bulbs - in borders	150mm	40 approx
Bulbs - naturalizing	scatter	10

Notes:
- Trees - tall = over 15m ultimate height
  - Medium = 8m to 15m ultimate height
  - small = under 8m ultimate height
- Shrubs - vigorous = only for the most vigorous, e.g. large buddlejas
  - medium = almost all shrubs including all large and medium evergreen shrubs
  - small = small hebes and cistus, etc., plants that ultimately grow to 1m spread

Notes on plant spacing

1. Specimen trees are drawn with a circle showing whether large, medium or small but with space left around for ultimate growth.
2. Avenues of trees are drawn as circles for the ultimate size of the tree but the circles set out so that there will always be space between adjacent trees and across the path or drive.
3. Specimen shrubs planted in grass need at least 2000mm spacing.
4. Wall shrubs, to be trained, are drawn as a half circle against the wall or fence allowing a 1500mm or 2000mm diameter depending on the size of the shrub.
5. Hedges are drawn as a series of linked circles, the centres of which show the spacing and the circles the clipped size of the mature hedge.
6. Small herbaceous plants planted at 300mm are usually too small to use as border plants so I rarely include this size circle unless drawing planting plans for herb gardens or alpine beds.
7. The spacing of ground-cover plants often depends where they are to be planted, as most of them will ultimately fill a 600mm area; however, when planted at the edge of a border, I place them at 450mm to get a quick cover and leave the same plant at 600mm in the centre of the bed, particularly when the area is also planted with trees and shrubs.

8. Climbing plants are shown as 2000mm or 3000mm long tubes, 300mm wide drawn along the wall with the cross showing where they are planted. On a pergola I just show a small circle around the cross in the planting position. It is almost impossible to write the name of the climber within the tube or circle so I write it as close as possible.
9. Herbs will vary in size depending on whether the herb is a shrub, an herbaceous perennial or an annual.

I have used these spacings for over 25 years, as I have always practised what I preached, and I still believe that these spacings hold true for almost all plantings. But of course there are exceptions, for instance, show gardens where plants need to be placed pot-thick. There is always the problem about clients wanting instant results, and the solution is to keep to the same spacings but purchase more mature, larger plants. Several of my clients who are keen gardeners sometimes prefer the choice of buying smaller plants and waiting for them to grow to fill the space. With some other gardens for which I am responsible, the soil is so well looked after, as are the plants, that it is possible to place plants at wider spacings because they quickly grow to their maximum size. I originally spaced shrubs at 1000mm adjacent to each other, but found that they quickly outgrew their locations, and had to be thinned — which destroyed the balance of the planting. So I now space the larger shrubs at 1500mm apart, with herbaceous plants or smaller shrubs between: thus the shrubs have room to grow to their full potential, and they will then crowd out the smaller plants.

Working without planting plans

It takes time to draw an accurate planting plan, but it is the only way to ensure that you get the result you want. The other alternative is to draw up a list of plants and then place all the plants yourself before planting. The only time I use this approach is when planting bedding schemes in a random pattern. I work out the dimensions of the beds and the number of plants needed, divide up the range of plants into this number, and then place them all out myself or use gardeners who understand the process. I would also use this process with some of the more naturalistic plantings including:

- wildflower meadows,
- bulbs in long grass,
- prairie planting — this may be sown as a seed mix rather than planted.

Style and pattern of planting

Before starting to fill in the planting plan, you need to decide on the style and pattern of planting for that particular bed. It will depend on the type of plants chosen to a certain extent, but not entirely. Annuals, bedding plants, roses and herbs can all be formal or informal, and adding a clipped box hedge around any planting will make it more formal. Planting used to be mostly in formal patterns or in regular groups of plants, but in recent years new styles of planting have emerged that need a different approach. So there are now at least three styles of planting including:

Formal pattern — rose beds,
— bedding,
— herb garden,
— parterres and knot gardens.
Informal groups — herbaceous borders,
— mixed borders,
— ground-cover planting.
Drifts — woodland planting,
— ground-cover planting.

There is a fourth approach to planting labelled **Matrix planting**. There has been much written about this method, but I find it all rather confusing — let alone time-consuming — because it would seem to be a more random style of planting bunched together with either ecological, naturalistic or new-wave planting. For me, matrix planting would be planting to a pattern, possibly contained in a grid, as I might use in planning a tree belt, where the pattern of planting was to be repeated.

Formal pattern

Plants are arranged in lines, blocks or a formal pattern. The design can be very simple like a chequerboard of squares, or very complicated as in some parterres. Formality was traditionally used for parterres, knot gardens and bedding, but now there are some really attractive new ideas using grasses and herbaceous plants.

Informal groups

This is the traditional approach to planting herbaceous and mixed borders. It is still very effective when done well, and can be high- or low-maintenance depending on the choice of plants and the size of each group. The latter should have the same visual impact, and to achieve it I use the ratio of 1:3:5 when deciding on the number of plants to use in each group.

Let me explain my 1:3:5 rule for planting. When creating my design I want each plant species to have the same value as the others. The easiest way is to give each plant species the same space, so if a shrub has to fill a metre of space, three plants spaced at 600mm apart are needed to fill the same space, or five plants spaced at 450mm apart to fill it too. In larger borders I may use a group of three shrubs which covers 3 metres, while plants 600mm apart would be in groups of nine, or those 450mm apart would be in groups of fifteen.

This is not a hard and fast rule and I vary the numbers where there is not enough, or too much, space.

Figure 7.6 The 1 : 3 : 5 rule for grouping plants.

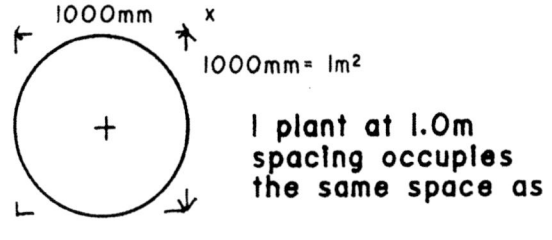

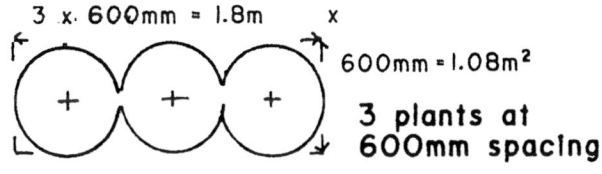

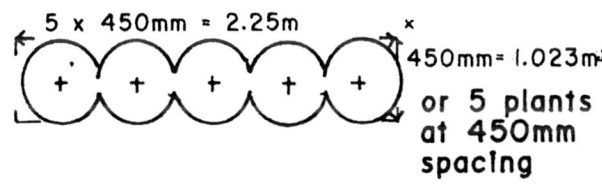

Figure 7.7 Part of a planting plan showing the plants arranged in groups of 1, 3 and 5.

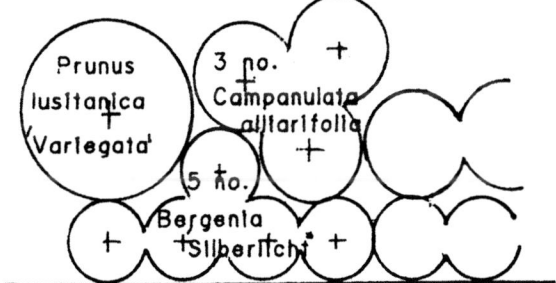

Drifts

These are much larger plant groupings with up to 50 or more plants of the same species in each group. With woodland planting the drifts may be organized according to the amount of shade, and with wetland planting according to the level of moisture.

Placing plants on the plan

At this stage, I begin filling in the planting plan with pencil circles of the right size for the range of plants chosen and, having decided on groups, drifts and numbers of plants in the groups or drifts, I start encircling these on the plan which, in turn, shows me how many different plants I am going to need. It makes planting plans more manageable when you know you need only seven front-of-border plants, or only 10 different drifts of ground-cover plants.

Also at this stage, I will draw up a list of plants that might be used on the plan (see the Chapter 6 on selecting plants).

I then start adding the names and numbers of the selected plants to the planting plan. You can do this randomly, but I find the following approach helpful as a useful starting point:

a) *If climbers are to be used*, I start by placing them at the back of the border spaced at a minimum of 2m apart; there are two approaches to using climbers:

   1. *As a background to cover the wall or fence with green* — in this case select a suitable plant with green leaves and medium or fine texture, and plant a row of the same plant along the length of the wall or fence.

   2. *As part of the chosen colour scheme*, but remember that climbers can easily unbalance a border because of their size and impact. The vertical cover of an individual climber is often far greater than the horizontal dimension of the border plants, so avoid very bright colours and bold foliage, which will tend to come forward and dominate the planting scheme. Nevertheless, coloured-leaf climbers can provide a background which co-ordinates with the colour scheme, and those with small flowers and foliage can work well.

b) *Position any large shrubs and wall shrubs*, if included, and allow room for their ultimate growth. Do not underestimate this, and place them far enough back in the bed or border so that, if left unpruned, they will remain within the planted area.

c) *Place front-of-border plants*, and choose plants which are low-growing with an attractive texture that will cover the ground. I consider that these are important plants, as usually I do not feel that bare soil is part of my planting scheme, and I also like to have a green frame to contain my plantings. I plant in groups of at least five plants, usually at 450mm apart.

d) *Select the plants for the back of the border*, shrubs may be planted singly but herbaceous plants should be in groups of three or more plants. Plants are selected to give height and structure so they are chosen for shape and habit of foliage and flowers.

e) *Fill up the centre of border* with herbaceous plants, roses or small shrubs of medium height, chosen for the colour impact of foliage and/or flowers. Plant in groups of at least three plants at 600mm apart or five plants at 450mm apart, depending on the ultimate size of the plants.

f) *Follow your colour scheme* and repeat with plants of same species or with different cultivars of the same species.

g) *Repeat shapes and habits* as well as colours and textures.

h) *Check the balance of colours and heights*.

When your planting plan is complete, prepare your plant list carefully checking that the numbers and names agree on the plan and the list.

Proposed plant list for ground-cover bed
Shady site with neutral loam soil
Foliage to be matt or hairy

Brunnera macrophylla 'Hadspen Cream'
Geranium macrorrhizum 'Variegatum'
Geranium x monacense 'Muldoon'
Geranium nodosum
Helleborus argutifolius
Helleborus foetidus 'Wester Flisk'
Heuchera cylindrica 'Greenfinch'
X Heucherella alba 'Bridget Bloom'
Lamium galeobdolon 'Florentinum'
Pulmonaria mollis
Pulmonaria saccharata
Symphytum 'Goldsmith'
Tellima grandiflora 'Purpurea'
Tiarella cordifolia

Stages in preparing a planting plan for a ground-cover bed

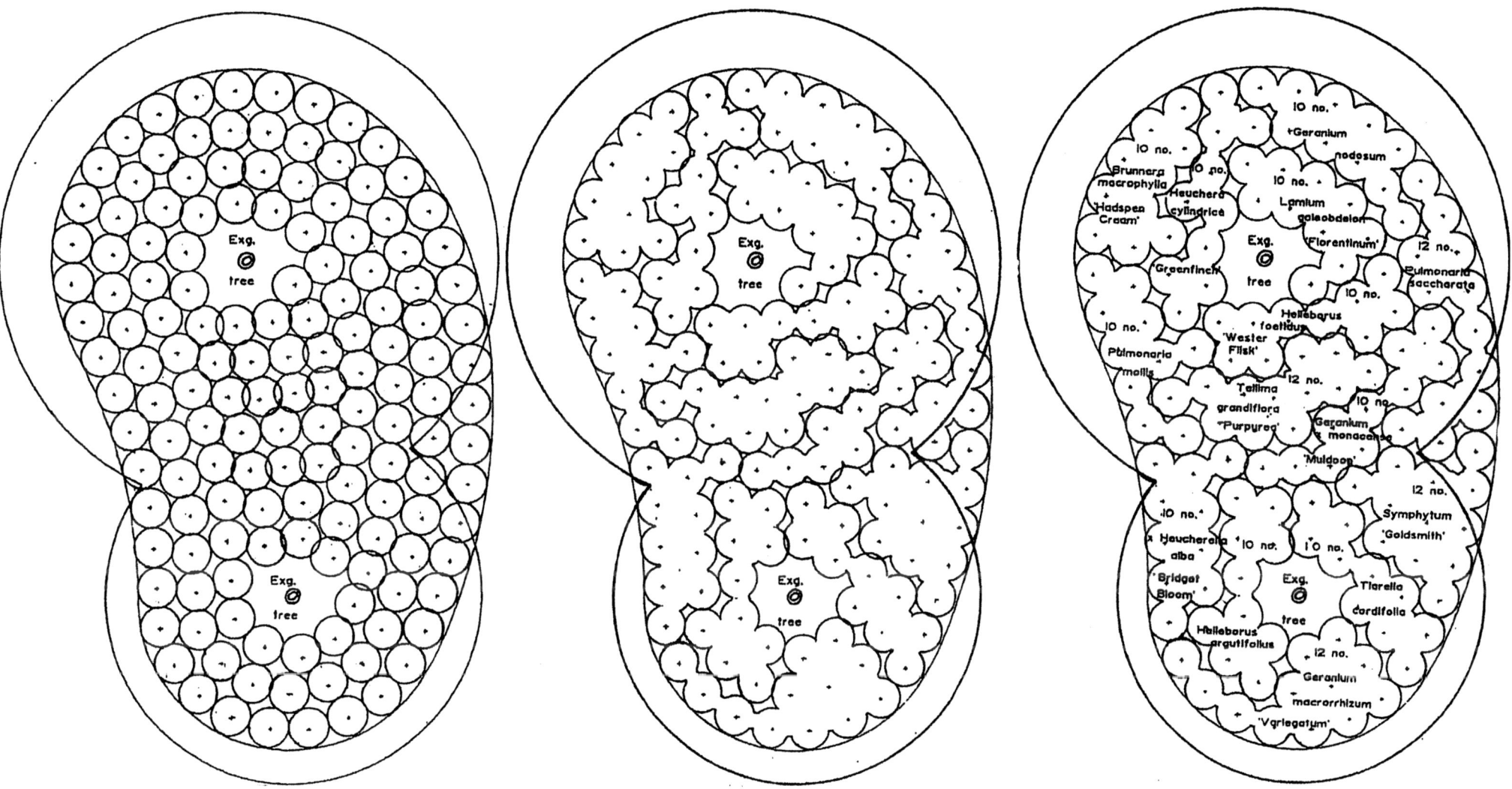

Figure 7.8 Stage 1: fill an outline of the bed with circles at 450mm spacing and include trunk and canopy of existing trees.

Figure 7.9 Stage 2: link circles in drifts of approximately ten plants.

Figure 7.10 Stage 3: add plant names and numbers to each drift of plants.

A view of the border in July.

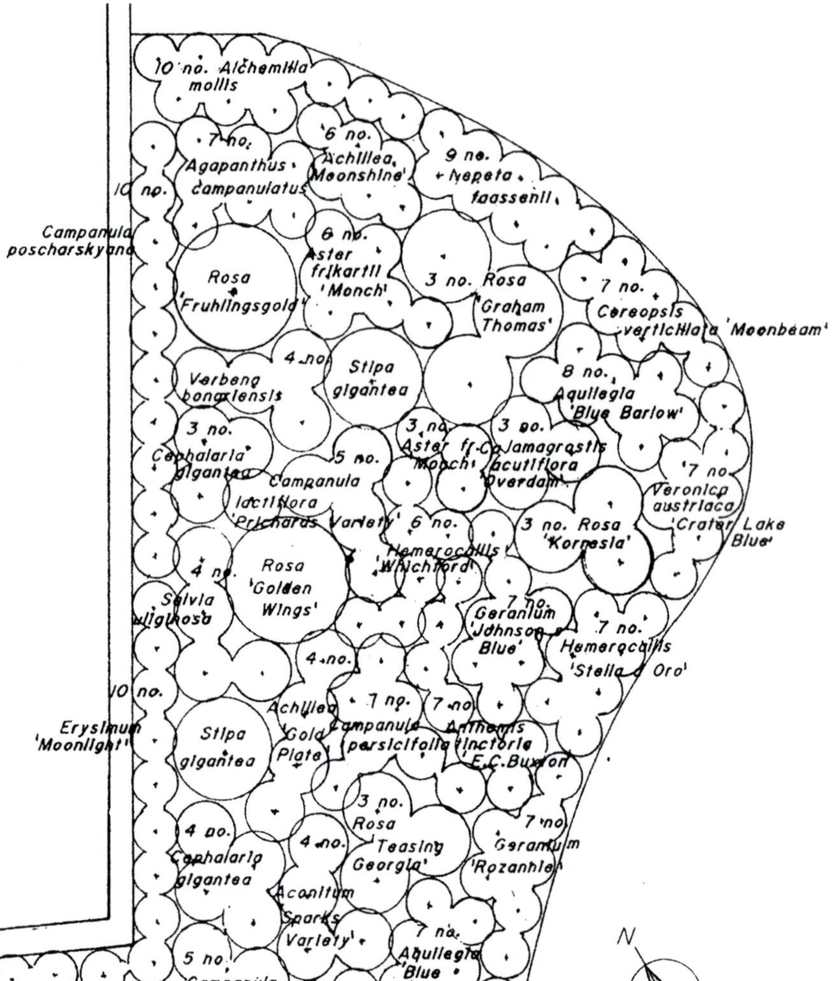

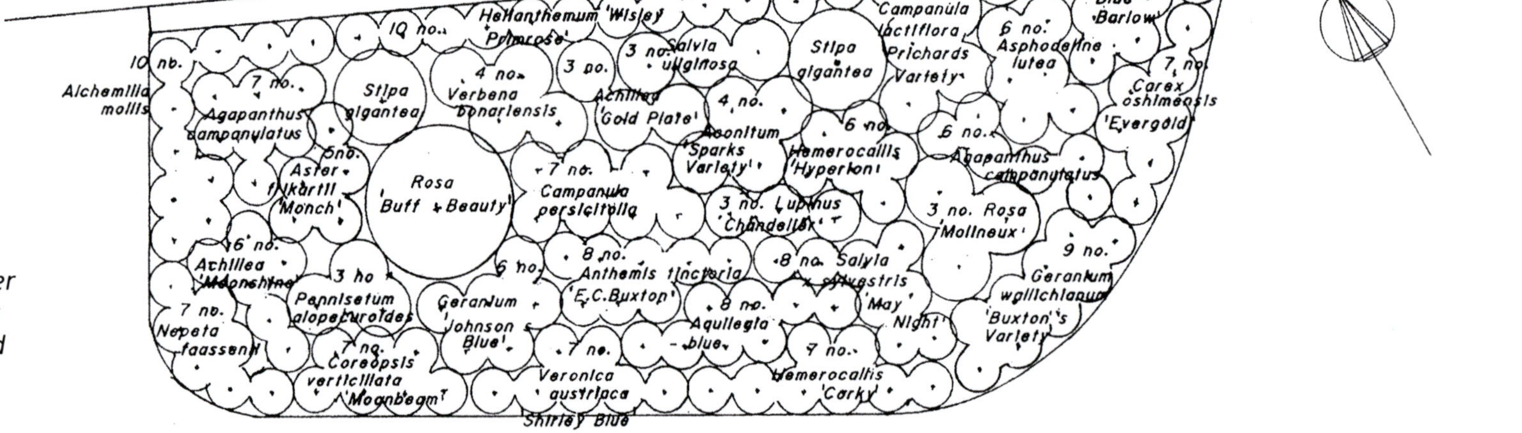

Figure 7.11 Planting plan for a yellow and blue border.
The border backs on to a ha-ha, and the client requested that the taller plants be light enough to see the deer park beyond. The plan was originally drawn at 1 : 50 but has been reduced to fit into the available space.

92 PLANTING PLANS

Plant Lists

The plant list, or plant schedule, is usually part of the contract documents and, again, must be clear and accurate. It is a list of the number and names of all the plants included on the plan or, where there are several planting plans, all the plants included in the planting to be done at any one time. It provides a shopping list for the contractor, client or gardener, and may be divided into the following types of plants:

1. Trees,
2. Conifers,
3. Shrubs,
4. Hedging plants,
5. Climbers,
6. Roses,
7. Herbaceous plants/ground cover,
8. Grasses and bamboos,
9. Ferns,
10. Water plants,
11. Bulbs,
12. Annuals.

The numbers of these which are included will depend on the area to be planted, and the size of the list. Ground-cover plants can be listed separately, or included with the shrubs and herbaceous plants.

Each section of the list needs to be in alphabetical order with the number and name of all plants included on the planting plans. The quantity is usually given as '12 no.' rather than '12 x', as the 'x' can be confused as part of the plant name. The name should be the correct botanical name, and I use the current copy of the *RHS Plant Finder* as my reference. In cases where the plant list is part of a contract, the size of the container to be supplied needs to be added or, where bare-root or root-balled plants are required, the size of the plant as well. Planting designers need to be familiar with all the available sizes of any particular plant, so that they are not caught out requesting a 14-16cm standard tree when the tree specified is only ever available as a half standard or in a container. If using an unfamiliar contractor, it may be advisable to give the size of the plant as well as the container to avoid being supplied with recently potted-up plants of inadequate dimensions.

With very large planting projects, I provide the contractor with two lists, one which is the total of all plants to be ordered and a second list with the same details but sub-divided into the different beds or planted areas to help the contractor in setting out the plants before planting.

All planting lists need to include the drawing number or numbers of the planting plan or plans to which they refer.

Plant list for groundcover bed

All plants to be supplied as 2-litre plants

10 no.	*Brunnera macrophylla* 'Hadspen Cream'
12 no.	*Geranium macrorrhizum* 'Variegatum'
10 no.	*Geranium x monacense* 'Muldoon'
10 no.	*Geranium nodosum*
10 no.	*Helleborus argutifolius*
10 no.	*Helleborus foetidus* 'Wester Flisk'
10 no.	*Heuchera cylindrica* 'Greenfinch'
10 no.	*X Heucherella alba* 'Bridget Bloom'
10 no.	*Lamium galeobdolon* 'Florentinum'
10 no.	*Pulmonaria mollis*
12 no.	*Pulmonaria saccharata*
12 no.	*Symphytum* 'Goldsmith'
12 no.	*Tellima grandiflora* 'Purpurea'
10 no.	*Tiarella cordifolia*

Planting specifications

These may also comprise part of the formal agreement with a contractor and list the work to be undertaken and the way in which the various operations are to be carried out.

They may be part of the overall specification for the landscaping of the site or as a separate document. Stand-alone planting specifications need to cover the supply and planting of the plants, and possibly their aftercare.

A useful reference for writing specifications is *Spon's Landscape Handbook*, edited by Derek Lovejoy; the 4th edition was published in 1997 but is still readily available. There are also British Standards for plants and planting which include:

BS3936-1:1992 Nursery stock. Specification for trees and shrubs.
BS3936-2:1990 Nursery stock. Specification for roses.
BS3936-3:1990 Nursery stock. Specification for fruit plants.
BS3936-4:2007 Nursery stock. Specification for forest trees, poplars and willows.
BS3936-7:1989 Nursery stock. Specification for bedding plants.
BS3936-9:1998 Nursery stock. Specification for bulbs, corms and tubers.
BS3936-10:1990 Nursery stock. Specification for ground-cover plants.
BS3936-11:1984 Nursery stock. Specification for container-grown culinary herbs.

BS4428:1989 Code of practice for general landscape operations covers planting.

Some designers just write in the specification plants to be supplied as BS3936 and planted as BS4428 without knowing exactly what is stated in these standards. So before including them in your documents, read the standards for yourself or write your own clauses as to how you want the plants supplied, how they are to be planted and any aftercare to be carried out.

Summary

How to achieve successful planting:

- Select plants for the soil, aspect and drainage of the site;
- Create attractive plant combinations using the visual qualities of each plant;
- Prepare clear planting plans and plant lists;
- Use good quality plants, and plant at the right time of the year where possible;
- Create planting schemes which can be maintained within the labour and skills available.

The colourful stems of Arbutus *'Marina' provide a framework for the sunlit grasses beyond.*

BOOK LIST

Rather than including a bibliography, I thought it might be more helpful if I listed the books to which I constantly refer and which sit next to my drawing board. Some I have had for many years, so they may well be out of print. Others I have added more recently, but all are used constantly as reference books.

If I look at these books, what singles them out is the fact that all of them are written by plant experts who have actually grown, or seen grown, all the plants they describe. So many books are written by garden writers who just copy information on plants from other books and do not actually know the plants they are writing about.

The list is in order of publication date as this is usually when I acquired my copy,

Plants for Ground Cover by Graham Stuart Thomas, published by Dent in 1970, was the first book on this subject and included planting distances amongst the other information. My well-worn copy demonstrates how much I have referred to it over the years, and still do.

The Readers' Digest Encyclopaedia of Garden Plants, published by The Readers' Digest Association in 1971, was the first modern encyclopedia of plants, full of invaluable information on the whole range of plants plus lots of illustrations; the list of contributors is a veritable 'who's who' of plant experts at the time.

Trees for Town and Country by Brenda Colvin, originally published in 1947; I bought the fourth edition in 1972. It is a great reference for using native and parkland trees.

The Hillier Manual of Trees and Shrubs, published in paperback by Hilliers in 1973, was an expanded version of their catalogue and includes details of 8000 plants.

The Hillier Manual of Trees and Shrubs, published in hardback by David and Charles the 1990, replaced my paperback which was falling to pieces. There is now an updated version of the Manual published by David and Charles in 2002, which includes 1500 extra trees and shrubs, and should be on every planting designer's bookshelf

The Hillier Colour Dictionary of Trees and Shrubs, published by David and Charles in 1981, contains details of only 3500 plants, but includes some useful illustrations.

Right Plant, Right Place by Nicola Ferguson, published by Pan Books in 1986, is a useful book when I am lost for a plant for a particular site like dry shade.

The Gardener's Illustrated Encyclopaedia of Trees and Shrubs by Brian Davis and published by Viking in 1987. Brian had been running a large commercial nursery for over 25 years when he wrote this book, and all the 2000 plants mentioned were those he had grown and were available commercially at the time. Apart from the wealth of useful information he gives on each plant, including soil, aspect, drainage and hardiness, he also notes any problems in growing it, which I have found invaluable.

The Kingfisher Guide to Garden Plants by Brian Davis, published by Kingfisher in 1988. The plants included are herbaceous plants and, again, all necessary information is given plus planting distance, problems and aftercare. My frustration with this book is that the plants are included by season and not alphabetically, which means using the index to find out where to find the plant I am looking for and whether it is in the book. An updated version was published in 2002.

The Gardener's Illustrated Encyclopaedia of Climbers and Wall Shrubs by Brian Davis, published by Viking in 1990, includes all the same useful information as his book on trees and shrubs.

The Royal Horticultural Society Gardeners' Encyclopaedia of Plants and Flowers, published by Dorling Kindersley in 1989, was an improvement on the Readers Digest Encyclopaedia because it prints 1000s of photos of the plants included. The problem is that the photographs are displayed by type or colour and not alphabetically, which means that you need to use the dictionary at the back to locate the plant you want.

Ornamental Shrubs, Climbers and Bamboos by Graham Stuart Thomas published by John Murray in 1992, is another mine of information, but sadly includes only a few black-and-white photographs to show the plants he describes.

The Royal Horticultural Society A-Z Encyclopaedia of Garden Flowers, published by Dorling Kindersley in 1996, is a book I use all the time. The only drawback is that it was originally published in a single volume which is incredibly heavy; it usually sits on the floor under my drawing board for this reason. Subsequently the RHS sensibly decided to publish it in two volumes, which are much easier to handle.

Christopher Lloyd's Garden Flowers by Christopher Lloyd and published by Cassells in 2000. Although it is not as useful as the enclyclopedias, I just love this book as it is full of the author's personal comments on each plant mentioned, gleaned from his lifetime working on the garden at Great Dixter.

RHS Plant Finder 2013–2014, published for the Royal Horticultural Society by Dorling Kindersley, is essential for getting plant nomenclature correct including recent name changes, and is also useful for checking on plant availability. Since it was first produced in 1987, it has been updated annually and now includes over 70,000 plants and details of which nurseries stock them. I replace my copy with the latest version every three to four years, and in selecting plants I try to keep to those that are quoted as 'widely available' in the book.

It's time for trees by Mike Glover and published by Barcham Trees in 2009. This is actually a catalogue for Barcham Trees, but the hardback is a great source of information, particularly on some of the newer tree cultivars now available

Trees for your garden by Nick Dunn published by The Tree Council in 2010. I have just found this book and I instantly sent for a copy as it is full of information, has great photos and includes fruit trees. Nick Dunn's family have run Frank Matthews' nursery for over 100 years and Nick has grown all the trees he includes.

Catalogues

I find some nursery catalogues almost as good as reference books, and sometimes quicker to find the information I am seeking. Those I update regularly include:

Handbook of Roses from David Austin Roses.

Seed and Plant Catalogues from Ball Colegrave. I am responsible for various bedding schemes and these catalogues keep me up to date with the latest bedding plant cultivars.

I also have a variety of bulb catalogues including J. Parker and Blom's bulbs which again I refer to for bedding schemes.

Web Sites
I have to confess that I prefer books but I increasingly use Google to find photographs of new cultivars.

RHS.org.uk is a mine of accurate information and includes the *RHS Plant Finder*, which saves buying the book if you enjoy going on line.

The **RHS plant selector programme** should be very useful, but it does not include some quite common plants such as sisyrinchium, but then has a range of less frequently grown cultivars: for example, there are five plants listed under eucomis. I would suggest it is intended for amateur gardeners, not professional garden designers.

I also use Palmstead Nurseries' site **Palmstead.co.uk** to check sizes and availability of plants as they are almost next door and I can visit the nursery to check the quality.

Davidaustinroses.com is a user-friendly website with plenty of information about each rose, so a valuable alternative to looking at their catalogue. I find this the easiest website to use for roses.

I have tried many other nursery websites, but I usually find them frustratingly hard to navigate to find what I am looking for. I then give up and go back to the books and catalogues on my shelves.

A word of warning
As I mentioned at the start of this section, I only use books written by plant experts; on the web the authorship of plant information is usually missing, so you cannot rely on this unless you are looking at a nursery's website where the plants described have been grown by them.

INDEX

Alps, landscape colours 60
arboretum 66, 67
arching habit 44, 46
Australia, landscape colours 55, 56, 60
autumn colours 52, 59
avenues 14, 15, 32, 66, 69, 70
axis, axes 10, 14

backgrounds 6, 23, 33, 36, 65, 90
beds, flower 16,17, 34-35, 90
   raised 29
bell-shaped plants 38, 39
borders 23, 26, 34-36, 89
boundaries 7, 15, 70
box hedges 5, 17, 30, 35, 36
Britain, landscape colours 53, 61
bulbs 19, 79

canopy, tree 66
carpet bedding 16, 17, 18
client brief 3
climbing plants 35, 71-72, 74, 88, 90
colour 37, 51-62, 92
   harmonies
      adjacent 51-54
      natural 60
      opposite, complementary 55-56
      tints, tones, shades 56
      triads 56-58
   seasons & sunlight 59
   spectrum 51, 52
   white 58
columnar shapes 38, 39, 40, 66
composition 10
cone shapes 40, 41
conifers 41, 48, 63, 67-69
cordons 29

daisy-shaped flowers 42
design
   factors 2
   harmony 9
   lines & shapes 3, 10, 13
   process 3, 11
   scale & proportion 10
   simplicity 9
   unity 9
dome-shaped plants 38, 39, 44
downland 20 *also see* wildflower meadows
drifts, planting 19, 20, 33, 75, 89, 91

ecology 20
espaliers 29

fan shapes 40, 41
'fedges' 13, 41
fleur-de-lis shaped flowers 42
focal points, planting 10, 22, 33, 39, 41, 44, 45, 67, 70
   backgrounds to 23
   enhancement viii, 22, 33
foliage
   coloured & variegated 22, 52, 66, 90
form, plants 37
   and *see* shape
fruit 7, 29
functional
   plan 4
   planting 5, 27

gardens
   cottage 63
   formal 14, 16, 27, 70, 89
   informal 14, 27, 70-71, 89

gazebo 22
grass
   long 18, 19, 33
   mown 13, 16, 18, 33
grasses 44, 78
green wall 13
ground-cover planting 16-21, 33, 68, 90-91
   formal 16-18
   informal 18-20
   natural 20-21, 33
   quasi-natural 20-21

habit, shrubs & trees 22, 37, 43-47
   arching 43, 44, 50
   horizontal 43, 45
   pendulous 43, 44
   prostrate 43
   tortuous 43, 45
   upright 43, 44
   weeping 43
harmony 9, 49 *also see under* colour
heathland 20
hedges 5, 7, 14, 23, 30, 36, 41, 68, 70-71
   box 5, 17, 30, 35, 36
   native shrubs 30, 31
herbs 27, 30
horizontal habit 43, 45

impact, flowers 63

knot gardens 18, 33

lawns 13, 16, 18, 33
leaf textures 47-50, 63
low-allergen garden i, 1

maintenance 24, 27, 36

Mediterranean landscape colours 54, 60
moisture levels 20
mood 13
moorland 20
mowers, grass/lawn 18, 19, 33
mowing strip 18

native vegetation 3, 7, 30, 65, 67
noise reduction 7, 28

obelisks 39
Olympic Park, London 19
orchards 67
ornamental planting 21, 24, 34, 68, 71
oval-shaped plants viii, 38, 39

parterres 17, 33
paths 25, 33, 66
   grass 33
   woodland 33
pendulous habit 43, 44, 66
plans
   functional 4
   mistakes 85
   plant lists 80, 90, 93
   presentation 8, 65, 83
   planting 83-94
   scales 83
   survey 4
planting
   background 23, 34, 36, 65
   beds 34-35, 89
   borders 23, 26, 34-36, 89
   boundary 15, 70
   bulbs 19, 33, 79
   carpet bedding 16, 17, 18
   composition 10, 22

design factors 2
drifts 19, 20, 33, 75, 89, 91
ecological 20
foliage colour 22, 52, 66, 90
food 7
formal 16-18, 27, 89
functional 5, 27
ground cover 16-21, 33, 68, 90-91
harmony 9, 49
herbaceous 63 *also see* plants -
    beds & borders
impact 63
knot gardens 18, 33
matrix 88
naturalistic 20-21, 33
ornamental 21, 24, 34
parterre 17, 33
pattern 88-89
positioning 89-90
prairie 21
quasi-natural 20-21
rose beds 56
screen 6, 15, 27, 28
seasonal 24
simplicity 9
spacing 86-88
    1:3:5 rule 89
structural 13-15, 30
types 27
unity 9
wildflower meadows 19, 20, 21, 27
plants, selection 65, 80
    annuals & biennials 79
    beds & borders 76-77, 90, 91, 92
    bulbs 79
    climbing 35, 71-72, 74, 88, 90
    conifers 67-69
    drifts 75,
    ferns 79

grasses & sedges 44, 78
ground cover 75
hedges 31, 68, 70-71
herbaceous perennials 76
roses 72-74
shade 78
shrubs 69-70
stream-side 86
trees 65
wetland 76
woodland 75
plants
    colour 37-62
    habit 37, 43-47
    height 87
    shape 22, 37-42
    size 37, 62-63
    texture 47-49
    visual qualities 37-50, 51-64, 80-82
pleaching 15, 28, 41
potager 29
prairie planting 21
privacy 7
prostrate habit 43, 46
pruning 41

Rocky Mountains, landscape colours
    60
roses 56, 72-74
rosette habit 46
round-shaped plants 38

saucer-shaped flowers 42
scales, plans 10, 27, 83, 86
screens, plant 6, 15, 27, 28
sculpture, living 45
seasonal planting 24, 59
seats 23

shade 7, 19, 20
shapes, plant & flower 22, 37-42
    bell 38, 39
    columnar 38, 39-40, 66
    cone 40, 41
    daisy 42
    dome 38, 39, 44
    fan 40, 41
    fleur-de-lis 42
    leaf 48 *and see* texture
    oblong 41
    oval viii, 38, 39
    round, spherical 37, 38, 39, 42
    saucer 42
    spiky 40, 41
    square 40, 41, 42
    tabular 40, 41
shelter 6, 7, 28, 63, 65, 68, 69
shrubs 36, 63, 69, 70, 90
    evergreen 69
    specimen 33
    upright habit 43
site survey 3-4
size 62-63
    leaf 48
    plants 37
slopes 33
space
    delineation 13
spacing, plant 86-88
specifications & standards 93-94
spiky shapes 40, 41
spring colours 52
square shapes 40, 41, 42
styles, house & garden 27, 63
summer-houses 10
sunlight 59
sunset colours 52, 53

tabular shapes 40, 41
texture, leaf 47-50, 63
tortuous habit 43
trees
    arboretum 66, 67
    avenues 14, 15, 32, 66, 69
    as background 23, 65
    belts, shelter 6, 28, 63, 65, 68
    canopy 66
    conifers 41, 48, 63, 67-69
    focal points 63, 65, 66, 69
    fruit, orchards 7, 29, 67
    naturalized planting 20
    pleached 15, 28, 41
    structural planting 13, 63, 65
    upright habit 43
trellis 13
tropical colours 55, 60

unfurling habit, ferns 46
upright habit 43, 44
urban landscaping 2

vegetables 5, 7, 29
views 6
vistas 10, 15, 70

walls 36
    green 13, 41
weeds, weeding 24
weeping habit 43, 66
wetland 20, 76
wildflower meadows 19, 20, 21, 27
wind 7
woodland 20, 75
    paths 33
woodland edge 20, 75

PLANT LIST

Acanthus spinosus 38, 82
Acer campestre (field maple) 31, 65
   A. cappadocium 'Aureum' 66
   A. davidii 40
   A. japonicum 40
   A. lobellii 38
   A. palmatum var. *dissectum* 'Red Autumn Lace' 48, 84
   A. platanoides 48
   A. p. 'Royal Red' 66
Alchemilla mollis 34, 76, 81
Achillea filipendula 'Gold Plate' 77
   A. millefolium (yarrow) 21
Aconitum carmichaelii 'Arendsii' 77
Actaea simplex 38
Aegopodium podagraria 'Variegatum' 82
Agapanthus campanulatus 77
Aeonium 'Zwartkop' 46
Alchemilla mollis 76
Allium christophii 82
   A. 'Purple Splendour' 37
Alnus cordata 38
   A. glutinosa (alder) 65
   A. incana 'Pendula' 66
Amelanchier arborea 'Robin Hill' 32
Anemone x hybridus 'Honorine Jobert' 77
   A. nemorosa 75
Angelica archangelica 38, 39
Anthemis tinctoria 'E.C. Buxton' 76
Aquilegia cvs 42, 82
   A. 'Blue Barlow' 77
Arbutus andrachnoides 47
   A. glandulosa 'Marina' 94
ash see *Fraxinus*
aspen see under *Populus*

Asphodeline lutea 78
Asplenium scolopendrium (hart's tongue fern) 79
Aster x frikartii 'Mőnch' 77
Asteraceae family 42
Astrantia major 82
   A. m. 'Hadspen Blood' 76
Aucuba japonica 69

beech see *Fagus*
Bergenia cordifolia 48
   B. 'Silberlicht' 76, 78
Betula nigra (birch) 40
   B. pendula (silver birch) 65
   B. pendula 'Youngii' 66
   B. pubescens (brown birch) 65
bluebell see *Hyacinthoides* 19
Brunnera macrophylla 38
   B. m. 'Hadspen Cream' 90, 93
   B. m. 'Jack Frost' 78
Buddleja davidii 40
Buxus sempervirens (box) 5, 17, 22, 35 41, 69, 71

Calamagrostis x acutiflora 'Overdam' 78
Calluna vulgaris (heather) 20, 75
Calocedrus decurrens 69
Camellia japonica 69
Campanula lactiflora 'Loddon Anna' 77
   C. persicifolia 42, 77
   C. punctata 38
   C. trachelium 38
Campanulaceae family 42
Carex elata 'Aurea' 78
   C. oshimensis 'Evergold' 78

C. 'Silver Sceptre' 78
Carpinus betulus (hornbeam) 5, 23, 30, 65
   C. betulus 'Fastigiata' 32
Castanea sativa (sweet chestnut) 32
Catalpa bignonioides 38
   C. b. Aurea' 66'
catmint see *Nepeta*
Cedrus atlantica 69
   C. libani 40, 45, 69
Centaurea Montana 40
Cephalaria gigantean 78
Cercis silliquastrum 38
Chamaecyparis lawsoniana (Lawson's cypress) 40, 68
   C. l. 'Columnaris' 69
   C. pisifera 'Boulevard' 68
Chamerion angustifolium 'Album' 40
cherry see under *Prunus*
chestnut see *Castanea*
Choisya ternata 38, 69
Clematis Montana 72
Cordyline australis 'Torbay Red' 70
Coreopsis grandiflora 76
Cornus Canadensis 75
   C. controversa 'Variegata' 22, 40, 45, 70
   C. kousa 40
   C. sanguinea (dogwood) 31
Cortaderia selicana (pampas grass) 78
Corylus avellana (hazel) 31
Cotoneaster dammeri 46, 75
   C. frigidus 'Cornubia' 69
   C. 'Hybridus Pendulus' 70
cotton lavender see *Santolina*
crab apple see *Malus*

Crataegus laevigata (Midland hawthorn) 65
   C. l. 'Paul's Scarlet' 32
   C. monogyna (hawthorn) 30, 31, 65
   C. persimilis 'Prunifolia' 32
Crocosmia 'Lucifer' 77
x *Cuprocyparis leylandii* (Leyland cypress) 68
Cyrtomium falcatum 79

Darmera peltata 63
delphinium 38
Deschampsia cespitosa 'Bronzeschleijer' 78
   D. flexuosa 'Tatra Gold' 78
Dicentra formosa 78
Dierama pendulum 46
dogwood see under *Cornus*
Dryopteris affinis 79
   D. filix-mas 79

Echinacea purpurea 38, 77
echinops 38
Elaeagnus x ebbingei 69
elder see *Sambucus*
elm see under *Ulmus*
Epilobium angustifolium 'Album' 77
Epimedium 47
   E. perralchicum 'Frohnleiten' 78
Eremurus bungei 38
Erica carnea 48, 75
Eryngium cvs 40
Erythronium dens-canis 'Pagoda' 81
Euonymus europaeus (spindle) 31
   E. japonicus 69
Euphorbia amygdaloides var. *robbiae* 78

E. characias 81
E. c. 'Tasmanian Tiger' 80

Fagus sylvatica (European beech) 30, 32, 48, 65
   F. s. 'Dawyck' 66
   F. s. 'Pendula' 66
   F. s. 'Riversii' 66
   F. s. f. purpurea (copper beech) 22
Festuca glauca 78
field maple *see under Acer*
Filipendula ulmaria (meadowsweet) 76
flag *see under Iris*
forsythia 40
Fraxinus excelsior (ash) 65
   F. e. 'Pendula' 66

Galium odoratum 75
Gaultheria shallon 75
Geranium himalayense 'Gravetye' 76
   G. macrorrhizum 50, 75
     G. m. 'Variegatum' 90, 93
   G. x monacense 'Muldoon' 90, 93
   G. nodosum 78, 90, 93
   G. phaeum 'Samobor' 78
   G. pratense 'Purple Heron' 64
   G. renardii 76
   G. sanguineum 76
Geum 'Borisii' 76
Gingko biloba 40
guelder rose *see under Viburnum*
Gunnera manicata 47

hazel *see Corylus*
hawthorn *see Crataegus*

heather *see Calluna*
Hebe albicans 38
   H. 'Mrs Winder' 64
Hedera colchica 72
   H. helix (ivy) 33, 71, 75
Helenium 'Moerheim Beauty' 77
Helleborus argutifolius 90, 93
   H. foetidus 'Wester Flisk' 90, 93
   H. x hybridus 78
Hemerocallis 'Gentle Shepherd' 77
Heuchera cylindrical 'Greenfinch' 90, 93
   H. 'Plum Puddin' 76
x *Heucherella alba* 'Bridget Bloom' 90, 93
holly *see Ilex*
honeysuckle *see Lonicera*
hornbeam *see Carpinus*
Hosta fortunei 38, 40
   H. 'Honeybells' 78, 82
   H. sieboldiana 48
   H. undulata var. *albomarginata* 82
Hyacinthoides non-scripta (bluebell) 5, 53
Hydrangea anomela subsp. *petiolaris* 72
Hypericum calycinum 75

Ilex x altaclarensis 69
   I. aquifolium 48, 69
Iris foetidissima 78
   I. germanica 42, 77
   I. pallida 'Variegata' 78
   I. pseudacorus (yellow flag) 76
   I. sibirica 50

Jasminum officinale 72
Juniperus communis (juniper) 67

J. horizontalis 75
J. scopulorum 'Sky Rocket' 38, 69

Knautia macedonica 77, 78
Kniphofia 'Little Maid' 78

Lamium galeobdolon 19, 75
   L. g. 'Florentinum' 90, 93
   L. maculatum 75
   L. orvala 78
Lavandula angustifolia (lavender) 71
Leucanthemum maximum 'Esther Read' 77
Leycesteria Formosa 40
Ligustrum lucidum 69
Liquidambar styraciflua 40
Liriodendron tulipfera 40
Liriope muscari 78
Lonicera japonica (Japanese honeysuckle) 72
   L. nitida 75
Luzula sylvatica 'Marginata' 78
Lythrum salicaria (purple loosestrife) 76

Magnolia grandiflora 38, 39, 48, 49
Mahonia japonica 69
Malus sylvestris 65
   M. tschonoskii 38
meadowsweet *see Filipendula*
Melianthus major 48
Miscanthus sinensis 'Morning Light' 78
Molinia caerulea 78
Monarda spp. 38
mountain ash *see under Sorbus*
Myosotis 'White Ball' 82

Nepeta x faassenii (catmint) 76
Nigella damascene 79

oak *see under Quercus*
Oreganum onites 'Aureum' 76
Osmanthus heterophyllus 69
   O. h. 'Purple Shaft' 64
Osteospermum jucundum 'Compactum' 42, 76

Paeonia lactiflora 77
   P. officinalis 37
Pachysandra terminalis 33
pampas grass *see Cortaderia*
Papava orientale 'Perry's White' 77
Parthenocissus quinquefolia (Virginia creeper) 71, 72
pear *see under Pyrus*
Penstemon 'Andenken an Friedrich Hahn' 77
periwinkle *see Vinca*
Persicaria bistorta 40
Petasites japonica 48
Phalaris arundinacea (gardener's garters) 78
   P. a. 'Feesey' 78
Phillyrea angustifolia viii
Phlox paniculata 77
   P. p. Norah Leigh' 77
Phormium cookianum 70
   hotinia x fraseri 'Red Robin' 69
Pinus mugo 38
   P. sylvestris (Scots pine) 45, 67
   P. wallichiana 68
Platanus x hispanica 32
Platanus orientalis 40
   P. nigra 'Italica' 38
Polemonium caeruleum 76

Polystichum aculeatum 79
   P. setiferum 79
Populus x canescens (grey poplar) 65
   P. nigra (black poplar) 65
   P. tremula (aspen)
Prunus avium (gean or wild cherry) 65
   P. a. 'Plena' 32
   P. dulcis 59
   P. 'Kanzan' 40
   P. laurocerasus 49, 69
   P. lusitanica 69
   P. padus (bird cherry) 65
   P. 'Pink Perfection' 32, 66
   P. spinosa (sloe) 31, 65
   P. subhirtella 'Autumnalis' 59
Pulmonaria mollis 90, 93
   P. saccharata 78, 90, 93
Pyracantha cvs 91
Pyrus calleryana 'Chanticleer' 32
   P. communis (pear) 38, 65

Quercus coccinea
   Q. petraea (sessile oak) 65
   Q. robur (pedunculate oak) 65
   Q. r. 'Fastigiata' 38

Ranunculaceae family 42
Ranunculus acris (buttercup) 21
Rheum palmatum 48
Rhododendron ponticum 38, 45
Rodgersia podophylla 48
Rosa spp. 73-74
   R. 'Albertine' 74
   R. arvensis (field rose) 73
   R. canina (dog rose) 73
   R. glauca 73
   R. 'Gloire de Dijon' 74

R. 'Just Joey' 73
R. moyesii 73
R. paulii 73
R. rugosa 31, 42, 73
R. spinosissima 73
R. 'Summer Dreams' 35
R. 'William Shakespeare' 74
Rosaceae family 42
Rowan *see under* Sorbus
Rubus tricolour 75
Rudbeckia fulgida 'Goldsturm' 19, 77, 81

Salix alba (white willow) 65
   S. caprea (goat willow) 31
   S. fragilis (crack willow) 65
   S. c. pendula 'Kilmarnock' 43, 66
   S. x sepulchralis var. *chrycosoma* (weeping willow) 22, 43
Salvia nemorosa 'Ostfriesland' 76
   S. officinalis 48
Sambucus nigra (elder) 31
Santolina chamaecyparis (cotton lavender) 71
Scabiosa caucasica 77
Sedum spectabile 'Brilliant' 76
   S. telephium 'Purple Emperor' 80
service tree *see under* Sorbus
silver birch *see under* Betula
Sisyrinchium striatum 76, 78
sloe *see under* Prunus
Sorbus aria (whitebeam) 32, 38, 65
   S. aucuparia (rowan or mountain ash) 65
   S. 'Joseph Rock' 32
   S. torminalis (wild service tree) 65
spindle *see under* Euonymus
Stachys byzantina 48

Stipa calamagrostis 78
   S. gigantea 78
Symphitum officinale 75
   S. 'Goldsmith' 90, 93

Taxus baccata (yew) 67
   T. b. 'Dovastoniana' 69
   T. b. 'Fastigiata' 39, 69
Tellima grandiflora 'Purpurea' 90, 93
Teucrium chamedrys (wall germander) 71
Thalictrum aquilegifolium 77
Thuja orientalis 'Aurea Nana' 38
   T. plicata 68
Tiarella cordifolia 90, 93
Tilia cordata (small-leaved lime) 65
   T. c. 'Greenspire' 32
   T. platyphyllus (broad-leaved lime) 65
Trachelospermum jasminoides 72
Trachycarpus fortunei 40
Tradescantia x andersoniana 77
Tulipa cvs 40, 61, 62, 64, 79

Ulmus glabra (wych elm) 65
   U. procera (English elm) 65

Verbena bonariensis 77, 78
Veronicastrum 'Temptation' 77
Viburnum davidii 38, 48
   V. lantana (wayfaring tree) 31
   V. opulus (guelder rose) 31, 39
   V. plicatum 'Mariesii' 45, 70
   V. rhytidiphyllum 49
   V. sargentii 'Onondaga' 70
   V. tinus 69
Vinca minor (periwinkle) 75

wall germander *see* Teucrium
whitebeam *see under* Sorbus
willow *see under* Salix
Wisteria floribunda 72

yarrow *see* Achillea
yew *see* Taxus
Yucca filamentosa 'Bright Edge' 70

Zantedeschia cvs 40